Cody, Matthew W., 1974-.
  Calvin Klein.

**FAMOUS
FASHION
DESIGNERS**

CALVIN KLEIN

FAMOUS
FASHION
DESIGNERS

COCO CHANEL

MARC JACOBS

CALVIN KLEIN

RALPH LAUREN

STELLA McCARTNEY

ISAAC MIZRAHI

VALENTINO

VERSACE

FAMOUS FASHION DESIGNERS

CALVIN KLEIN

Matt W. Cody

CHELSEA HOUSE
An Infobase Learning Company

For Daniel, always in style.

CALVIN KLEIN

Chelsea House
An imprint of Infobase Learning
132 West 31st Street
New York NY 10001

Library of Congress Cataloging-in-Publication Data

Cody, Matthew W., 1974-
    Calvin Klein / by Matt W. Cody.
       p. cm. — (Famous fashion designers)
    Includes bibliographical references and index.
    ISBN 978-1-60413-979-2 (hardcover)
    1. Klein, Calvin, 1942–   —Juvenile literature. 2. Fashion designers—United States—Biography—Juvenile literature. I. Klein, Calvin, 1942- II. Title. III. Series.

    TT505.K58C63 2011
    746.9'2092—dc22
    [B]   2010034102

Text design and composition by Lina Farinella
Cover design by Alicia Post
Cover printed by Bang Printing, Brainerd, Minn.
Book printed and bound by Bang Printing, Brainerd, Minn.
Date printed: February 2011
Printed in the United States of America

10 9 8 7 6 5 4 3 2 1

Contents

1

An American Classic

One afternoon, you decide to take a walk through the four-level, 20,000-square-foot (1,858-square-meter) Calvin Klein store on Madison Avenue in New York City. It is a powerful experience because everything about the store says *Calvin Klein*. It is an immense open space. You're nearly overwhelmed by the extremely high ceilings. The lighting is carefully controlled. Neutral colors meet your eye. The walls are colored cream, tan, and beige. The clothing racks are sparsely stocked. Shelves of neatly folded shirts are accented with other Calvin Klein products—wooden salad spoons, pewter bowls, eyeglasses, and 18 different kinds of men's and women's colognes. The clothes themselves are classic Calvin Klein: soft, natural fabrics in subtle, neutral colors. There is an intensity to the calmness of your surroundings.

Calvin Klein's brand has become synonymous with elegance and simplicity.

And yet, for all the signs that you are in a thoroughly "Calvin Klein-esque" environment, today you notice a few subtle signs that things may be changing in the world of this classic American designer. As you walk through the women's collection on the main floor, you suddenly see a flash of fuchsia. You begin your tour of the men's collection on the top floor and you're greeted by a pair of shiny, silver shoes. Never mind that they cost several hundred dollars; you smile because they are so witty and fun. Among the rows and rows of black suit jackets, pale gray sweaters, and khaki pants, you spy T-shirts of a vivid turquoise. A trip to the lower level where the Calvin Klein Home collection is displayed holds similar surprises. You aren't surprised to see tan sheets and pillowcases, but what about that tall glass bowl in a shade of eggplant purple?

LEADER OF A GLOBAL EMPIRE

These unexpected, colorful moments signal a shift in a company that has consistently maintained the vision of one man for more than 40 years: Calvin Klein. The story of how this middle-class Jewish boy from New York City became one of the most iconic American fashion designers of all time and went on to lead a global, multibillion-dollar design empire is a tale of skill, luck, perseverance, and unrelenting self-promotion.

Calvin Klein's designs are world famous and instantly recognizable. Words used to describe his style include *modern, clean, sleek, practical, sensuous,* and, above all, *American.* Beyond his fame as a designer, Klein is well known as a master of marketing. Over his long career, Calvin Klein created a brand that has become synonymous with both quality and controversy. Whether he was being praised for his creative vision or criticized for his notorious advertisements, people were talking about Calvin Klein. As fashion historian François Baudot says, "Far more than a mere fashion company . . . Calvin Klein is a multi-product worldwide phenomenon, whose exposure to the media is second to none."

DESIGNER OR IMAGE MAKER?

Calvin Klein came along during a period of change in the fashion industry. American fashion designers were challenging long-established French couturiers with sporty, casual looks. Klein's own design style was unmistakable: classic, well-tailored clothes made from fine, natural fabrics in colors that were muted and subtle. His clothes were "easy, pure and simple," fashion writer Jane Mulvagh has said. Women loved how his modern, sensual designs felt on their body. "I make clothes people like to wear," Klein said, and this remark sums up his legacy. Klein is the ultimate example of a designer whose clothes reflect less of a personal artistic vision than what he felt people liked to wear. Fashion historians may argue about whether Klein's view of the fashion design business was, in the words of one of his biographers, "more business than art and design," but either way, his place in fashion history is secure. Although Klein no longer controls the company that bears his name, it will likely endure because the name has come to represent style, elegance, and quality to millions of people around the globe.

2

Beginnings

Calvin Richard Klein was born November 19, 1942, in the Bronx, one of five boroughs that make up New York City. The Kleins were just one of many Jewish families who lived in the neighborhood. These families had survived the Great Depression, and they respected hard work and the value of a dollar. The neighborhood was somewhat divided between the affluent and the middle- and lower-classes, which made some people overly aware of their social status. The wealthier families lived along a ritzy street called the Grand Concourse. Calvin's family resided in a lower- and middle-class area called the Mosholu Parkway. Owning a home was expensive, and most families, including Calvin's, lived in large apartments that could comfortably accommodate a family.

CALVIN AS A BOY

Calvin and his family enjoyed a lifestyle typical for a middle-class Jewish family of the time. They attended a synagogue that had many prominent Jewish families as members. (In a fascinating coincidence, future superstar designer Ralph Lauren and his family went to the Kleins' synagogue.) Calvin attended a public elementary school in his neighborhood. While he did well in all subjects, he had a particular passion for art class. In fact, he was gifted for his age. He designed all sorts of amazing projects, including a large mural that he painted on a wall near the principal's office. By the time he was in his early teens, Calvin was traveling into Manhattan every Saturday for drawing classes at the Art Students League of New York. The Art Students League was established more than 130 years ago by a group of artists who wanted a place to teach classes in drawing, painting, and sculpture. The Art Students League still exists today.

While he would eventually grow into a trim, athletic man about six feet, two inches (188 centimeters) tall, Calvin was a very skinny—one might even say scrawny—little boy. He had light brown hair, hazel eyes, and a face spotted with freckles. Shy but with varied interests, including pet lizards, turtles, and parakeets, he loved one hobby more than any other: designing and sewing clothes. His interest in clothes appeared at a very early age because of two women: his mother and his grandmother.

TWO EARLY INFLUENCES

Klein's mother was named Flore (pronounced "Flora"), but everyone called her "Flo." By most accounts, Flo was a passionate and gregarious (some would say overbearing) woman. She absolutely loved clothes and went shopping frequently. "My mother was a very strong character," Klein told *Vogue* magazine. "She dressed very elegantly." Some pieces of Flo's wardrobe were so fancy—she owned a fur stole made of real mink—that she stood out among other mothers in the neighborhood. Not all of her clothes were pricey, however. One of the places where Flo loved to shop was a discount department store named Loehmann's. Young Calvin loved going there with his mother and was utterly fascinated by the selections she made.

Flo's mother (Calvin's grandmother) was a seamstress so talented that many felt she could have had a career as a dress designer. "Molly," as she was called, was an emigrant from Austria. She came to the United States around the turn of the twentieth century and married a dentist named Max Stern. Max (Calvin's grandfather) had a gambling problem, and Molly had to take seamstress jobs just to make up for the income that Max gambled away. The problem became so bad that eventually Max left Molly and she had to raise their children all alone.

Calvin loved his grandmother and especially respected her sewing abilities. Calvin would sit and watch her sew beautiful gowns at her sewing machine. One year, Calvin received a sewing machine as a birthday present because his mother noticed how entranced he was with his grandmother's creations. Soon everyone recognized that Calvin's interest in sewing women's clothes was more than a hobby. He had the makings of a professional dressmaker. Calvin was teased at school for not being interested in sports like the other boys, but he wasn't discouraged. "At age five I had a pretty good idea of what I wanted to do," said Klein years later. Calvin's mother supported him enthusiastically. Where other boys his age were encouraged to become doctors and lawyers, Flo bragged about her son's enormous talents for sewing and designing to anyone who would listen.

THE KLEIN FAMILY

Flo Klein was definitely the boss of the Klein family, which included Calvin's older brother, Barry, and their younger sister, Alexis. Flo could be a rather controlling mother, and she liked to demonstrate that they could afford expensive material things, even if they couldn't. For example, the family owned a washing machine and several air conditioners, all extravagant purchases for the 1950s. Each of her three children wore expensive clothes and had his or her own telephone. Flo had the most trouble with Barry, who, like his grandfather, got caught up in excessive gambling. With the painful memory of her father deserting her family never far away, Flo insisted that Barry quit gambling, but he refused. Her favorite was young Calvin, who never had to do the same chores his siblings did.

Calvin's father, Leo Klein, was an emigrant from Hungary. He was a typical 1950s father: honest, stern, and not emotionally expressive. Though the boy loved him dearly, Leo and Calvin's relationship remained distant throughout their lives. Those who knew the family say that Leo was not terribly pleased with his son's career choice, but, in the face of bossy Flo, he had little choice but to go along.

Leo was a grocer and for a while owned his own store in Harlem, a neighborhood in northern Manhattan. Eventually the store hit hard times and Leo had to close it. He was forced to go to work in his older brother Ernest's grocery store, Ernest Klein & Co. Flo, ever concerned with her social position, was jealous of Ernest Klein's success. She felt embarrassed by her family's lack of money in comparison to Ernest's. Adding to her envy and bitterness, Flo herself had to work at Ernest's store on occasion to help pay the bills. However, it was from watching his parents that young Calvin picked up the value of hard work.

A FRIEND FOR LIFE

Calvin's best friend was a boy named Barry Schwartz, and not only would they remain friends for the rest of their lives, but they would become business partners as well. Many felt it made sense that Barry had the same first name as Calvin's older brother, because the two boys were so close it was as if they were

Barry Schwartz attends New York City Fashion Week in 2001 with his wife, Sheryl. Schwartz brought his financial skills to childhood friend Klein's fashion business. Together, the two built a global empire.

brothers. Physically, however, they could not have been more different. Where the young Calvin was tall, thin, and scrawny, Barry was short, athletic, and tough. Calvin, wearing clothes picked out by his mother, always looked clean and polished. Barry hardly ever wore anything other than T-shirts and blue jeans. Calvin was stylish and Barry was not.

The boys did have many other things in common. First, they were neighbors; in fact, they lived only a few blocks apart. Second, they were both Jewish and studied Hebrew together in preparation for their bar mitzvahs. Third, they both loved movies, often attending a Saturday matinee at the magnificent Paradise movie palace on the Grand Concourse. Their most important shared interest, however, was their mutual ambition. Calvin and Barry both dreamed of becoming rich someday, and their entrepreneurial spirit revealed itself early on. The boys ran all kinds of little businesses in their neighborhood, like selling iced tea during the summer. Another plan was to buy the daily newspapers and then resell them at profits of a few pennies per paper. They were always talking about someday owning a chain of supermarkets or pet stores. The boys were dreaming big.

There were also some similarities between Barry and Calvin's families. Like Calvin's father, Barry's father was a grocer. Harry Schwartz's Sundial grocery store was in Harlem, and he was well liked among his neighbors, even remaining there through the years when Harlem was plagued with crime.

There was one more thing that Barry Schwartz and Calvin had in common: Barry's father, like Calvin's brother and grandfather, had a gambling addiction. Harry Schwartz liked to bet on horses and play dice. He ran a booking service out of the office in his grocery store. People would come and go all day, buying groceries or placing bets with Harry. They were hoping to strike it rich on the racetrack. Eventually, Barry became interested in gambling and would take Calvin with him to the racetrack.

ELEMENTS OF STYLE

I've always had one closest friend—Barry Schwartz. We've been friends for 36 years, since the age of five. If you really love someone and care about him, you can survive many difficulties, and there have been many difficulties in the relationship. . . . I try to understand how he lives. I live in the city; he lives in the country. He hates being in New York and wants to go home to his children, wants to be on the farm. . . . We have to understand and be tolerant of each other. It was a special friendship from the beginning, and it turned out to be the American dream. I wouldn't know what to do without him.

Calvin Klein in Playboy *magazine*

LEARNING ABOUT FASHION

When the boys were old enough to begin high school, Barry and their other classmates went to an all-boys school in their neighborhood. Calvin, however, had his eye on someplace else.

The High School for the Industrial Arts

The High School for the Industrial Arts (now called the High School of Art and Design) in Manhattan was a place where Calvin could study what he really loved: drawing and art. Attending the High School for the Industrial Arts required a long train ride into Manhattan every day. But Calvin was determined and committed. He hoped it would be a place where he could feel accepted by his peers, unlike his elementary and junior high schools. His hopes were realized as he began to meet the other kids who were just as artistic and "different" as he was. The students were asked to choose a main subject to study, and Calvin chose fashion illustration. Interestingly, Calvin did not see himself as becoming a fashion designer—he was still palling around with Barry, going to the horse track, and dreaming of making big money co-owning supermarkets with Barry as his partner.

At the High School for the Industrial Arts, Calvin learned sketching and other design techniques; however, he was still years from becoming a professional designer. One of his teachers, Olga Petroff, remembered Calvin in this way: "There were many talented students. . . . I wouldn't put him in the top group . . . yet he had the keen sense of judgment to know whether something was good or not. He had style more than great design. As far as real design, I never thought he had that."

Calvin's fellow classmates felt the same way. Most remembered Calvin not as a particularly talented designer but as someone with a strong ability to copy the styles of other famous designers of the time, like Christian Dior and Coco Chanel. In Calvin's defense, however, most young artists, be they fashion designers, actors, or painters, begin by mimicking the work of their heroes. Yet it was a critique that would stick with Calvin for the rest of his career.

FIT

After Calvin graduated from the High School for the Industrial Arts, rather than going to a traditional college or university, he stayed with fashion and started taking classes at the Fashion Institute of Technology, or FIT. Today, FIT is one of the most famous fashion schools in the world, offering classes on everything from fashion design, marketing, and illustration to computer animation and graphics. In 1960, however, it was thought of as an old-fashioned trade school. Most classes were in basic techniques like sewing and patternmaking, though as the decade went on, FIT would come to offer instruction in interior design and photography. Calvin, however, was bored. He wanted to learn the basics of the business, but he was anxious to get out into the real world and get started.

Ready-to-Wear

In the early 1960s, there were relatively few major fashion designers who were American. So while Calvin admired the great

Designer Claire McCardell puts the finishing touches on a suit in 1940.
As one of the first American ready-to-wear designers, McCardell
served as an inspiration to Klein.

European designers like Chanel and Dior, he lacked role models closer to home. At FIT, however, Calvin was lucky enough to study with one of the few American fashion giants of the day, Claire McCardell. McCardell was making a name for herself by developing collections of ready-to-wear clothes. In the years after World War II, there was a demand for clothes that could be bought at department stores and worn immediately. Finer than one's work wardrobe but not exactly fancy, ready-to-wear designs were, in the words of fashion historian François Baudot, "a comfortable and elegant way for modern women to dress." For

A Pioneer of Casual Fashion

Claire McCardell was the most influential member of a group of American designers who led the way in ready-to-wear designs. Born in Maryland in 1906, McCardell was the pioneer of casual, sporty, American looks that inspired generations of designers and, in particular, Calvin Klein. She specialized in separates, which are pieces that can be mixed and matched with others, like blouses and skirts. McCardell loved simple designs and essential fabrics like denim, rayon, and cotton jersey. Among her signature looks were ladies' pantsuits, sweaters with hoods attached, and dresses done in graph-paper-checked fabric. She was also one of the first to design dresses that allowed women to show their bare midriff. Indeed, many of today's most beloved casual designs began with Claire McCardell: wrap dresses, sundresses with spaghetti straps, and her "popover" dress, which was a denim wrap dress that could be worn during any season. McCardell achieved something rare: She was stylish and unpretentious at the same time. Calvin Klein remains her most ardent admirer. Of McCardell's clothes, Klein has said, "They are the only clothes from the late forties and fifties that could still be worn today beautifully."

example, a ready-to-wear dress could be slipped on over the head and pulled shut with a drawstring at the waist. Ready-to-wear fashions also sported fun patterns like stripes, checks, and plaids instead of traditional solids.

Claire McCardell was a big influence on Calvin in a number of ways. First of all, Calvin loved casual fashions just as much as the high-end gowns and dresses that got most of the attention in those days. Second, McCardell's color palette was largely made up of light, subtle shades like beige, gray, and tan. Muted colors like these would become one of Calvin's trademarks. He also loved McCardell's simple style. For example, she hardly ever used floral prints in her designs, and her pieces were free of accessories and busy detailing.

A KEEN EYE

FIT also provided Calvin ample opportunity to practice his most impressive ability: to judge the value of a design. While he was criticized for this talent in high school, it got him a lot of attention at FIT. Calvin became notorious for his strong opinions about both the work of his classmates and the fashions of the day. He began to develop strong likes and dislikes for certain fabrics, looks, styles, and colors. In 1963, Calvin earned his fine arts degree from FIT. Just 20 years old, he was about to find out whether there was place for him in the world of professional fashion design.

3

Starting Out

It was the early 1960s, and the professional fashion world was not one that today's designers would recognize. Though fashion design had a distinguished history, it was not yet accepted as an art form, especially not in America. Fashion writer Lisa Marsh describes the distinction this way: "American women [of the mid-1960s] wore *clothing—fashion* was something that came from the runways of Paris."

A BRIEF HISTORY OF FASHION

During the twentieth century, changes in fashion styles happened very quickly—at least once every decade. Trends originated either in New York or Paris. Paris had been and still was the fashion capital of the world. The fashions of the first years of the twentieth century were basically holdovers from the previous century. Dresses were ornate, lacy, and tightly fitted. Women had to wear corsets just to fit into them. Wealthier women could afford clothes made by a great Parisian couture designer like Paul Poiret or Jacques Doucet, or they might hire a local seamstress to copy and hand-sew a new French design.

The 1910s and 1920s

One of the first important changes in fashion was purely technical. Clothes that were mass-produced in factories were less expensive than couture, and so middle-class women began buying stylish clothes from mail-order catalogs. During the 1910s and 1920s, fashion magazines like *Vogue* and *Vanity Fair* became popular,

Coco Chanel

Of the leading French fashion designers of the 1920s and 1930s, one in particular stands out as an icon of the era: Gabrielle "Coco" Chanel. Born in France in 1883, Chanel had an early career as a concert-hall singer before becoming a fashion designer. She began as a hat designer and soon moved on to dresses and other womenswear. Chanel was responsible for numerous breakthrough designs at a time when women were desperately in need of them. Her overriding philosophy of women's clothes was that they should be comfortable. For example, she was an early champion of women's pants and pajamas. She also loved casual sportswear and created signature knit sweaters and pleated skirts—again, always emphasizing comfort over social appropriateness. Indeed, comfort was so important to Chanel that she once remarked that she wanted her clothes to offer women "the possibility to laugh and eat without necessarily having to faint." Chanel couldn't care less about long, one-piece gowns; even her cocktail dresses were in two pieces, with the skirt ending at the calf. In 1926, she too. Women could see pictures of the latest styles and fashions from Paris.

The style of the clothes themselves was changing, too. The tight-fitting fashions of the nineteenth century were being replaced by flowing dresses that did not require a corset. By the 1920s, the "flapper" look was in: dresses were cut above the knee, skirts were pleated, waists were dropped, and hems were trimmed with fringe, beads, and tassels.

Sportswear was also emerging as a popular choice for women. Knit pullover sweaters found their way into a woman's leisure wardrobe. The popularity of sportswear raised an important question that would remain relevant for years to come: What was more

designed the very first "little black dress," which remains an absolutely essential piece for many modern women. If that iconic piece weren't enough to secure Chanel's place in history, her iconic two-piece, wool jersey suit would seal the deal. A Chanel suit, "more a way of life than an article of clothing," claims writer Emma Baxter-Wright, was a picture of sporty, feminine simplicity. Chanel borrowed the suit look from men's fashion yet feminized it with short skirts, open-necked blouses, and flannel blazers. The suits were slim, spare, and unadorned, and the wool jersey fabric was the height of comfort (it had only been used for men's underwear up to that time). So though the suits were tightly fitted, they were soft to the touch. In her later years, Chanel was an important link between regular women's fashion and Hollywood. She was hired by MGM Studios in 1931 to costume movie stars and later designed for actresses Grace Kelly and Elizabeth Taylor. Fashion historians have linked Calvin Klein to Coco Chanel because they share two characteristics: a similar color palette of black, white, and beige and a passion for comfortable, sporty, ready-to-wear clothes. It must also be mentioned that Chanel's idea for her own perfume (famously named Chanel No. 5) was picked up by Klein as well. Fashion historian Gerda Buxbaum summarizes Chanel's lasting influence: "Almost all womenswear today, no matter what kind it is, is essentially the result of Chanel's ideas (and) experiments."

important to a woman, style or comfort? Some women could afford fabulous couture gowns, yet the dresses were not always very comfortable. Women who favored more comfortable clothing, however, looked less elegant. It was an issue that would drive the creation of the comfortable—yet fashionable—"ready-to-wear" designs of Coco Chanel, Claire McCardell, and Calvin Klein.

The 1930s

In the 1930s, women's fashion was influenced by a source that continues to hold considerable power today: Hollywood. The Golden Age of Hollywood, as the decade was called, brought increased awareness of women's fashion to a larger public. Actresses like Bette Davis, Katharine Hepburn, and Rosalind Russell became instant fashion icons, wearing dramatic, glamorous evening gowns made of shiny silk. Many 1930s gowns had halter necks, meaning they were looped around the neck, leaving the back and shoulders exposed. In the 1930s, the silhouette of a dress was more formfitting as women became comfortable showing their natural "hourglass" shape.

The decade of the 1930s was a time of great economic stress in America, and the fashion industry felt the impact. When the stock market crashed in 1929 and triggered the Great Depression, most American women could no longer afford what they could in the 1920s. As a result, they began buying clothes that were sturdy, practical, and easily mended. Casual wear continued to gain in popularity as women began wearing pants—as Katharine Hepburn was doing in the movies—and used accessories like pins, brooches, and earrings to make a simpler look appear more elegant.

In the 1930s, shirtwaist dresses were introduced. Sweaters were popular with women for the first time as well. Women also wore furs of every kind as capes, stoles, and coats. Busy prints influenced by the Cubist movement in painting (as in the works of Pablo Picasso) were also popular. Improved manufacturing techniques continued to affect fashion trends. Synthetic, or machine-made, fibers like rayon became popular because they were lightweight, wouldn't wrinkle easily, and could be washed.

In the 1920s, fashion changed considerably. Hemlines rose and clothing became less formfitting, as shown by this flapper. The manufacturing of clothing changed, as well, with mass-produced ready-to-wear garments replacing custom-made fashions.

The 1940s and 1950s

When World War II broke out in 1939 and America joined the effort in 1941, fashion changed almost overnight. First of all, the war created fabric shortages. Silk was needed for making parachutes and wool was needed for uniforms, so synthetic fabrics like rayon became even more popular. Second, the war seemed to call for greater modesty, simplicity, and functionality in clothes. Styles were inspired by the military look, and navy and gray tailored suits were popular with women. These suits sported straight, flat skirts, narrow lapels on the jackets, and shoulder pads. Dresses and gowns continued to be made during the war, but in a nod to the wartime economy, they tended to be day-to-night pieces that could be worn to all kinds of occasions.

The war also caused an important shift in the fashion capital of the world from Paris to New York. Because Paris was occupied by German soldiers during the war and therefore isolated from the rest of the world, American design houses, which had always looked to Paris for inspiration, had to go it alone. For their inspiration, American designers looked to two sources: people living in California and college students. In both cases, the fashions were casual and sporty. This new emphasis on comfort and leisure would be the hallmark of American fashion for decades to come.

After the war, the American economy boomed, and women were eager to set aside their wartime frugality and buy fashionable clothes again. Women were also entering the workplace in greater numbers, and they needed outfits for the office. A trio of New York–based designers—Claire McCardell, Jo Copeland, and Vera Maxwell—picked up where Coco Chanel left off and created classic American collections of simple, mix-and-match separates, like blouses, skirts, and tops. The pieces were functional and came in solids, prints, and patterns. They were made from softer fabrics like gingham and denim and could be bought "off the rack" in department stores or from mail-order catalogs. The fashion industry was beginning to take ready-to-wear fashions seriously. For example, the entire August 1955 issue of *Vogue* was dedicated to ready-to-wear designs. These American ready-to-wear designers were Calvin Klein's "ancestors." Klein would soon take sportswear to new heights.

MANUFACTURER-DESIGNERS

In the late 1950s and early 1960s, the whole idea of a "fashion designer" was unknown in America. In those days, a designer was someone who worked for a big fashion manufacturing company and sketched designs for the owner. For example, a man named Maurice Rentner was a well-known New York–based manufacturer-designer in the 1960s. Rentner had many designers working for him, and some, like Bill Blass, went on and become fashion designers in the modern sense. But in those days, if you read the label inside a Blass-designed garment, it would read, "Bill Blass for Maurice Rentner." It was the Rentner name that women in the 1950s and 1960s trusted. These women would shop for Rentner garments at large department stores like Bloomingdale's and Bonwit Teller in New York City.

Dan Millstein

Calvin Klein caught a big break when he was hired by one of New York's most well-established manufacturer-designers. His name was Dan Millstein, and he owned a store in New York's garment district. Since the earliest years of the twentieth century, New York's garment district, located on Seventh Avenue, had been the center of clothing manufacturing. It remains a hub of activity today, and the economy of New York City is greatly supported by the tens of thousands of jobs the garment district provides.

A tough, grumpy man who could be quite rude, Millstein's specialty was suits and coats for women. It was a rather dull area of the industry to be sure, but it provided some job security for Klein, who was just starting out. The Millstein store was elegant and glamorous, and Millstein himself was very wealthy. Klein was in awe of him. But Millstein was more of a "manufacturer," in Klein's words, than a designer.

Klein was hired as a sketcher for the store, which meant that his job was to draw on paper what another person, the "idea" person, came up with. Klein hated his job. He wanted to be the "idea" person! Yet Klein learned many things from Millstein that would serve him well in the future, such as the difference between a fine fabric and a cheap imitation made to look fine. Klein also noticed how expertly Millstein dealt with customers.

An American in Paris

One of the most significant events in Klein's early development occurred when Millstein took Klein with him to Paris to view the new fashion collections. Millstein was known for being the first American manufacturer-designer to travel to Paris each season for a look at the new fashion trends. In those years, American designers were allowed to go to fashion shows if they paid a fee and promised to buy some garments.

Klein was awestruck; he had never seen so much elegant clothing! Millstein put him to work right away sketching the designs that came down the runway. Incredibly, Klein was expected to do this from memory, because an open sketch pad would have certainly looked suspicious at a runway show. So Klein watched all the shows, memorized the designs, and later sketched them out from memory in his hotel room.

Something else important happened to Klein in Paris. While Millstein was copying French designs and passing them off as his own (common practice in those days), Klein was studying the clothes he was seeing regular people wear on the streets. He couldn't understand how the high fashions that Millstein loved would ever translate into clothes for regular Americans. Klein told *Playboy* magazine in 1984, "When I got out of school in the middle 1960s, [American designers] were considered inferior—copyists of the

ELEMENTS OF STYLE

[Dan] Millstein designed gaudy clothes: bright-yellow, orange and lilac suits with long-haired fox collars and cuffs that sometimes ran down the front of the three-quarter-length jacket and around the entire border of the suit. . . . I needed the job and had to design those suits, but fortunately, I never saw anyone wear one of them. Then, one day, I saw a woman walking down the street in the yellow suit with the yellow fox collar and cuffs, a yellow hat, a yellow handbag and yellow shoes—and I quit! I was sick to think that I had been part of making that outfit possible.

Calvin Klein in Playboy *magazine*

Europeans, lucky if we got a front-row seat at a French couture collection. I couldn't relate to what I saw in Paris, because the clothing had nothing to do with an American lifestyle; it tended to be formal, luxurious and a bit pretentious. American designers' clothes have a sense of reality, practicality and sensuousness."

A NEW PARTNER

Around the time that Klein was at Millstein's, he proposed to a young woman whom he had known since he was very young, Jayne Centre. Jayne had been a fellow student in elementary school and then again at FIT. Since leaving FIT, she had been working as a designer of textiles. Klein's mother, Flo, was thrilled that her shy son was finally going to get married. They had a lovely wedding in 1964 and found an apartment in the Forest Hills neighborhood of Queens, east of Manhattan. The early years of their marriage were fun and happy. Yet it was not easy being married to someone as driven as Klein. He was hardly ever at home. It didn't take long for Jayne to begin resenting how much Klein worked.

Then, in 1967, a wonderful thing happened. Calvin and Jayne had a baby girl. They named her Marci. Calvin adored her, but the numerous baby-related expenses forced him to work even longer hours. He rarely slept more than four hours a night. Jayne was already unhappy with her husband's workload. Even though he was doing it to support her and the baby, she became even more discontent in their marriage. They began to argue frequently.

Jayne was just starting to see a side of Klein that his friends and colleagues had known about for years. A shy man by nature, Klein has been described by some as passionate and ambitious, but by others as obsessive, perfectionistic, and workaholic. Klein once defended himself by saying that this side of himself is what

In the 1930s and 1940s, it became acceptable for women to wear trousers and other menswear, as popularized by film legend Katharine Hepburn (*above*). Klein would draw from these styles for many of his designs.

has made him successful: "When I want something, I give it everything I've got. With me, it's all or nothing."

HALLDON, LTD.

Frustrated with his low salary and lack of advancement, Klein eventually quit his job at Millstein's. When Klein quit Millstein's, it is said that Dan Millstein didn't even say goodbye. Klein next began working for a company named Halldon, Ltd. Halldon was well-known for its coats and, in particular, for its fake furs. Working at Halldon was different from working at Millstein's. Klein earned a good salary and was treated well.

At Halldon, Klein's talent for being able to evaluate and select the best designs was again noticed. The owner of Halldon reflected on this some years later: "I think Calvin's main talent was his selection of what the woman wants, that excellent feel of timing in the country and what will be accepted. . . . He knew communication. He knew how to handle people, and he could read people. He was brilliant in that department, no question about it." At Halldon, Klein became someone to watch. His coat designs, even for fake furs (which he loathed), were gaining admirers in the industry. One industry publication noted at this time that he was "one of the more aggressive and imaginative young coat and suit designers."

AN IMPORTANT DECISION

Yet Klein was restless and bored at Halldon, just as he had been at Millstein's. He wanted to be out on his own. He approached an old friend, Abe Morenstein, and discussed starting a business together. Morenstein, who thought Klein was an up-and-comer in the industry, agreed. Klein was still working at Halldon under a strict contract, so the two men had to keep their business plan secret. For three months, Klein sewed a sample collection of six coats and three dresses.

Starting a design business costs money, and Klein figured that they needed about $25,000. No matter whom they asked or where they looked, they simply couldn't raise the money. Just as it is today, the fashion district back then was full of young designers looking for people to invest in their designs. Deeply frustrated, Klein turned to his best friend, Barry Schwartz.

During the years that Klein had been at Millstein's and Halldon, Schwartz had been learning his father's supermarket business. One horrible day, the family store was robbed and Barry's father was murdered. Barry, then enlisted in the army, rushed home to attend his father's funeral. He was now responsible for his mother's well-being. Demonstrating the business skills that would eventually make him rich beyond his wildest imagination, Schwartz got to work and transformed the family grocery store into a thriving business.

A Generous Offer

Of course, Schwartz and Klein had been talking about owning a business together since they were boys. Years later, Klein recalled going to Schwartz for advice: "[Schwartz] knew how frustrated I was in my job and offered me a full partnership in his supermarket. He didn't want any money from me; he just wanted to help. Being married and being frustrated at work, I decided to seriously consider his offer." Klein was faced with a difficult choice: Go into the supermarket business with his best friend or stick with the fashion design business and try to raise money for his own line.

Klein even went to his father for advice, an uncommon act for him in those days. Klein recalled approaching his father: "I was convinced my father would say, 'Go into the supermarket business with Barry.' At dinner, he shocked me: 'I think you would be making a tremendous mistake,' he said. 'I don't understand what you've been studying all these years, but whatever it is, I don't think you've given it enough of a chance. If you don't continue with what you're doing, I think you'll regret it for the rest of your life.' I was surprised and very moved. He convinced me and was responsible for my making one of the most important decisions in my life—making the commitment to stick with fashion." Touched by his father's confidence in him, he politely told Barry thank you, but no thank you. He wanted to be a designer, not a grocer.

Incorporation

Upon hearing that from his friend, Schwartz offered Klein the first $10,000 needed to start the business. Klein was stunned by his friend's generosity. After some thought, Klein accepted the money, and on December 28, 1967, Calvin Klein, Ltd., was incorporated. Klein listed himself as half owner. The other half belonged not to Abe Morenstein but to Barry Schwartz. After all, Klein thought, it was Barry's money they were using to create the samples.

When Morenstein learned of this, he felt betrayed. It was bad enough, Morenstein felt, that the company did not bear any part of his name, but not even to have any ownership of it was the ultimate insult. Klein's decision caused a permanent rift in their friendship. The two men would not speak to each other for 24 years.

The rest of the fashion industry soon heard about Klein's new company. When word of Klein's secret collection reached the owner of Halldon, Klein was released from his contract. Calvin Klein was finally on his own.

4

The Birth of a Business

W hen he incorporated his new business in the late 1960s, Calvin Klein found himself in a world of fashion that was changing. Someday, Klein would be leading the way toward new fashion styles, but back then, he was just trying to keep up with all the trends.

1960s FASHION

The 1960s were an extraordinarily fluid and varied decade. Fashions turned into fads, meaning they changed quickly. Stylistic influences seemed to come from everywhere: from Parisian couture to American rock 'n' roll, from British movies to San Francisco hippies. Everything from miniskirts and caftans to hot pants and plastic raincoats came and went.

Perhaps the most important change of the decade was yet another shift, though temporary, of the fashion capital, this time from Paris to London. England was home to the new "mod" look popularized in British films like *Alfie* and *Darling* (and spoofed decades later in the *Austin Powers* movies); it consisted of mini-skirts, minidresses, and one-piece shift dresses that started at the neck and went all the way below the knee. In the United States, the most original designs came out of the hippie movement. Hippies were young people living in San Francisco and elsewhere who were against anything that represented the "establishment": the Vietnam War, the military, corporations, and even fashion. Their tie-dyed shirts, flower-print dresses, psychedelic tunics, second-hand wares, and denim blue jeans created a unique 1960s look.

MINIMALISM

Despite being surrounded by all these different styles, by the late 1960s, Klein was developing his own personal style, saying, "My buzz words have always been modernity, purity, neutral shades, a whisper of sex appeal and, most of all, minimalism." Minimalist design is characterized by refinement, restraint, and elegance. Minimalist clothes usually have classic silhouettes and tailoring with solid and subtle colors. Minimalist designers believe that "less is more." Calvin Klein is regarded as the leading minimalist designer of the second half of the twentieth century. Of Klein's minimalist style, *Time* magazine said, "... it's always about eliminating anything that is not necessary, and always thinking about the garment as being as pure as possible."

STARTING A BUSINESS

The constantly changing environment of the late 1960s was a challenging one in which to start a new business. Some long-established, family-owned dress shops in the garment district

This suit from a 1977 Calvin Klein collection epitomizes all that Klein stood for from the very beginning of his career: classic lines, minimalism, and modernity. Klein had the knack of putting a feminine twist—in this case a plunging neckline—on a menswear-inspired garment.

could not keep up with the times and closed. Yet Klein went full steam ahead and opened a small showroom. It was really tough. How could anyone keep up with all the changes in style? It seemed like every couple of months, a trend went out of style and was replaced by something else. Whatever people were buying, they weren't buying Calvin Klein. Money was running out fast, and Klein was alone—but not for long.

As Klein struggled to get his business up and running, Barry Schwartz was experiencing transitions of his own. In addition to recently getting married, he experienced a devastating loss. Following the assassination of Martin Luther King Jr. in April 1968, Harlem, a predominantly African-American neighborhood, went through a period of violent race riots. During one such riot, Schwartz's supermarket was almost totally destroyed. Faced with the daunting task of rebuilding his store from the ground up, Schwartz decided to go in another direction. He called Klein and told him that from that day forward, they would be business partners.

A LUCKY BREAK

Anyone who has ever started a successful business will say that it takes a lot of luck. Klein and Schwartz's lucky break was when the vice-president of Bonwit Teller, a big New York department store, happened to be in the building where Klein had his small space. His name was Donald O'Brien, and he was immediately impressed with Klein's designs, which he saw hanging in the doorway of Klein's tiny showroom. Cleverly, Klein had hung the garments there in the hopes that just such a person as O'Brien might notice them while waiting for an elevator. O'Brien invited Klein to meet the president of the company.

In a story that is now legendary, Klein personally pushed his garment rack up Seventh Avenue to the Bonwit Teller offices— just because he was so afraid his samples would get wrinkled in a taxi! Soon, Klein found himself in the office of Mildred Custin, the president of Bonwit Teller. Custin was a major force in

ELEMENTS OF STYLE

I was nervous about meeting [Mildred] Custin, because she was the major force in fashion at the time . . . she started the entire designer-boutique concept and was a true innovator in retailing. In short, the grande dame of the retail world! When I arrived in Custin's office, I held the samples up one at a time; she never smiled, just looked at them. . . . I don't think [my samples] were unique at all. What made them different was their youthful quality. The coat industry had been run by manufacturers who were in their 60s and 70s, whose products were very conservative. My clothes were understated, in very pretty colors and younger! I was 25 years old and thinking about the fact that young people needed coats, too. Believe me, there wasn't anyone doing anything young at that time.

Calvin Klein in Playboy *magazine*

the fashion industry. She had a reputation for finding the hottest new designers in America and Europe and then promoting them through her 12 Bonwit Teller stores across the United States. At first, Custin, a tough, elegant woman in her fifties, showed no enthusiasm for Klein's handmade pieces. Then suddenly, she turned to Klein and ordered $50,000 worth of dresses for her stores. Klein almost fainted. This was what he had been dreaming of—a big order from an important store! His dresses on sale at Bonwit Teller? It seemed too good to be true. Calvin Klein was about to be put on the map. Custin later said that "what impressed me the most was the purity of his line and the simplicity of his designs."

Bonwit Teller was just the beginning. Soon word got out that Mildred Custin had made another of her famous discoveries. Other stores fell in line—Garfinckel's department store in Washington, D.C., and I. Magnin in San Francisco, not to mention New

York institutions like Bergdorf Goodman and Saks Fifth Avenue. Suddenly, Klein and Schwartz had big orders to fill, and now they needed the actual clothes, which was no small task. Klein was realizing that there were about a million things to do before his clothes would appear on the racks in department stores all over the East Coast. Klein was unbelievably busy. He finally had to put a sofa in his office because some nights he slept in his office. Their entire enterprise was one big gamble. But Klein was confident; he knew he was talented. Plus, people were ordering his clothes, so he had no alternative but to just keep marching forward.

The fashion industry, for all its glamour, is at its core a business. In other words, Klein and Schwartz needed money—a lot of money. Every task had its cost. They had to find money to pay for everything from purchasing the fabric to hiring trucks to ship the finished garments to the stores. So they did what every small designer has to do when he or she is starting out: they borrowed. In addition to the $10,000 that Schwartz gave Klein to start, they went to a bank that promised to match Schwartz's donation if he added another $25,000, which he promptly did. Armed with $70,000, they were ready to begin manufacturing the order for Bonwit Teller.

A HIGH-PROFILE DEBUT

By this time, the fashion industry had realized that younger women were buying clothes that were very different than what their mothers were wearing. Younger women wanted pieces that were sleek and stylish, yet affordable. Custin had long wanted to introduce a line of clothing with just these traits, and in Klein she had the perfect designer. Custin, who praised Klein as an "American Yves Saint Laurent," decided that her newest discovery, still only in his twenties, was going to be the man behind this entirely new department of her store. Not only would Klein be featured in all eight of her Fifth Avenue storefront windows, but his new designs for young women would be shown in a big ad in the *New York Times*,

In the fashion industry, it is not enough to have talent. You must be able to promote your product. With the help of department store Bonwit Teller, Klein was heralded as the "American Yves Saint Laurent" while still in his twenties.

too. The new line made a huge splash, and orders began to roll in at a tremendous rate. It seemed as though Klein rocketed to the top of the industry almost overnight. In just its first year, Calvin Klein, Ltd., made a million dollars.

BECOMING A "NAME DESIGNER"

By the end of the 1960s, some American fashion designers were becoming famous. Women wanted garments created by "name designers" like Geoffrey Beene, Oscar de la Renta, and Bill Blass. While these men were not yet among the top high-end designers of the world—they weren't designing couture for movie stars, for example—they were all name designers. The level below them was made up of the unknown (and often unnamed) designers who made clothes that were sold "off the rack" in department stores. Up to this point, Klein was a member of this bottom group. Now that his line for Bonwit Teller had taken off, he desperately wanted to move up and be known as a name designer.

Being a name designer had its advantages. First, it was becoming more common for the name of the designer, not the store where it was bought, to appear on the labels of the clothes. Second, name designers had more control over their designs and were involved in day-to-day business. The days when a big store like Millstein's kept a designer like Calvin Klein in a back room were gone. A name designer would go in person to a store like Bonwit Teller and actually see what women were wearing and buying. You could get to know everyone at every level of the industry—the customers, the buyers, and the distributors.

ROMANCING THE PRESS

If he were ever going to become a name designer, however, there was one aspect of the fashion industry that Klein was going to have to master: publicity. As designers became celebrities, many fashion magazines covered them. Fashion journalists were now an integral part of the industry, and trade publications like *Women's Wear Daily* suddenly became a place to read all the latest news and gossip about fashion, fashion designers, and the famous women who wore them. When a movie premiered, for example, the dress that the leading lady was wearing that night was newsworthy. "Who

Yves Saint Laurent

Yves Saint Laurent, whom the *New York Times* called "one of the best-known and most influential couturiers of the second half of the 20th century," was a master French designer who revolutionized how women dressed and created some of the most iconic looks in fashion history. A 21-year-old Saint Laurent burst onto the fashion scene in 1957 when the great French designer Christian Dior suddenly died and Saint Laurent was named his successor. From his very first collection, Saint Laurent was a success. Though his time at Dior was brief, a career had been launched. He was one of the first French designers to launch a ready-to-wear line, in 1962, and it was truly distinctive. The designs were inspired by the art of Piet Mondrian, whose paintings were composed of primary-colored geometric shapes set against a white background, and accented with black lines. He also introduced iconic 1960s pieces like the see-through dress, the vinyl dress, the safari jacket, and the women's tuxedo. In the 1970s, Saint Laurent once again took his inspiration from a great twentieth-century painter, this time Pablo Picasso. His "Homage to Picasso" collection of 1979 consisted of wild prints that were in sharp contrast to his classic ready-to-wear collections of wools, knits, and linens. Saint Laurent was also a champion of the women's pantsuit and created a distinctive version made of denim. "My small job as a couturier," he once said, "is to make clothes that reflect our times. I'm convinced women want to wear pants." Saint Laurent was leading the way in fashion yet again in the 1980s, as his take on the women's suit, with a shorter jacket and fuller skirt, became the look that everyone copied, including Calvin Klein. In 1983, Saint Laurent was given a rare honor as a retrospective of 25 years of his work opened at the Metropolitan Museum of Art in New York. It was the first time the museum had honored a living designer in this way. When the designer died of brain cancer in 2008 at the age of 71, the fashion world was deeply shaken by the loss. His funeral was attended by a virtual who's who of fashion design, including Jean-Paul Gaultier, Vivienne Westwood, and Valentino.

you were wearing" became a symbol of one's fame and status. Even women who weren't celebrities wanted to own "a Bill Blass" or "an Oscar de la Renta."

Nothing was covered more extensively by the new fashion press than the yearly fashion runway shows where designers introduced their new collections. The fashion press was becoming so powerful that if designers wanted to have a successful launch of a new collection, they had to get good reviews—and they were not above scheming to do so. If you were a fashion journalist and you wanted to be invited to a designer's show next season, you had better give *this* season's show a good review. Klein told *Playboy*, "Politicking is certainly necessary with the press, with buyers, with the presidents of stores, with unions, with every-one a designer comes into contact with. You'd be a damn fool if you were out to fight the world and expected to succeed in it. I don't think there's anything wrong with politicking in order to get what you need."

Klein was a darling of the fashion press because his story was so compelling: "Boy from the Bronx makes it big!" He was a partic-ular favorite of the famous magazine *Harper's Bazaar*, and he soon began appearing in *Vogue* as well. Klein did nothing to discourage the publicity. The names and faces of other name designers were showing up in the magazines, and he wanted to be there, too.

EARLY CRITICISM

In the early years of Klein's career, many in the fashion press noticed how much he borrowed from the designs of Yves Saint Laurent. Early on, Klein would often copy Saint Laurent's designs, produce them more cheaply, and sell them for much less than Saint Lau-rent would. Yet the fashion press was critical of this practice, and soon Klein realized that his nickname "the American Yves Saint Laurent" was no longer a compliment. There was nothing wrong with being influenced by Saint Laurent, Chanel, and McCardell, but Klein needed to find a style of his own.

 One of Calvin Klein's signatures is putting a spin on a classic garment. Throughout his career, his aesthetic would remain essentially the same. The design worn by this model at a Calvin Klein show in the 1970s could just as easily have been shown today.

MENTORS

Around this time, two important figures entered Klein's life. Both were prominent figures in the fashion press. Eve Orton wrote about fabrics and furs for *Harper's Bazaar*. An older woman of considerable elegance and style, she took an immediate liking to the handsome young designer. Orton introduced Klein to a lot of important people in the industry. She was known for supporting new designers, as she had already done for Ralph Lauren. Her influence on Klein was so great that she actually enriched his style. For example, she showed him new ways to accessorize his fashions, both for fashion shows and for the department store racks. She also got him to consider colors outside of the rather neutral palette he had been using since his days at FIT. Many describe Klein's early work as downright drab before Orton arrived on the scene.

The other influence on Klein in these early years was another fur and fabric writer, this time for *Vogue*. Count Nicolas de Gunzberg, Klein would later say, was "a particular inspiration in my work. He was truly the great inspiration of my life from the time we met . . . he was my mentor, I was his protégé." A rare man in an industry dominated by women, de Gunzberg was an elegant gentleman in his sixties who had worked as an editor for both *Vogue* and *Harper's Bazaar*. He was originally from Paris, and, with his full head of silver hair, looked and acted like a king. His own personal style was extremely fashionable. He always sported the latest clothes.

Both Orton and de Gunzberg were close enough to Klein that he gave them a sneak preview of his new collections each season. De Gunzberg could be especially biting in his criticism, but it was always to help make Klein a better designer. He eventually went to work for Klein. Eve Orton was particularly valuable each season during Klein's runway shows. Today a runway show is a huge production, but in those early days, Klein would hire just four models to walk down a cheap set of risers. People sat on folding chairs and drank coffee and ate cookies. Klein would become a nervous wreck as the big day approached, and Orton was always brought in to make everything sparkle and shine a little bit more.

"A DESIGNER TO WATCH"

Calvin Klein's first runway show in the spring of 1970 has become something of a legend in the fashion business. If there were any doubt that a major designer had arrived on the scene, the reaction from the fashion and design press eliminated it. "A designer to watch," exclaimed *Women's Wear Daily*. The most popular piece in the show was Klein's version of a peacoat. A peacoat is a double-breasted outer coat with big buttons and lapels. Peacoats originally were worn by sailors. It was a move that would become characteristic for Klein: to take a classic piece and put an elegant, unusual spin on it. Klein's peacoat had a distinctive silhouette, a high collar, and eight buttons.

Looking back, perhaps the most fascinating aspect of Klein's first show was how fully it revealed his personal philosophy of design—a style that would remain essentially unchanged for the rest of his career. His garments were simple, subtle, and classic. Klein elaborated, "I don't think women should spend hours deciding what they should wear, and frankly, there are more important things to do with their money than putting it all into clothes." Yet however affordable his clothes were, they had style.

By the end of 1971, Klein's business had profited $5 million. He finally had enough money to fulfill another dream—to take over the office space of his old employer Dan Millstein. Millstein was a member of fashion's old guard, and he had struggled personally and professionally in the years since Klein had exited. He was suffering from cancer and his business was fading. Klein bought the space, and soon he was running his growing empire from the office of the man who had given him his start. To the very end, Klein maintained his opinion of Millstein as a tough, unkind, ruthless boss: "[Millstein] was an impossible man with a colossal temper." Now he was his own boss, seemingly ready to face the numerous challenges that lay ahead.

5

Becoming an Icon

In her book *Vintage Fashion*, author Emma Baxter-Wright remarks that the 1970s "was the decade in which ready-to-wear came into its own. Separates were a key component, instead of whole outfits in the formal couture sense. . . . 'Together but apart' was fashion's most wearable message yet." It makes sense, then, that the 1970s was also the decade when Calvin Klein began his meteoric rise to the top of American fashion design. Klein had a burning desire to create high-quality collections of elegant, comfortable, ready-to-wear classics for modern American women. What makes Klein stand out, however, is that he didn't stop there. By the end of the decade, he would branch out into unexplored areas, cementing his status as a great American designer.

This look, from Klein's 1975 Fall/Winter show, illustrates Klein's tendency to mix sumptuous natural fabrics, such as furs, tweeds, and silks.

AN "AMERICAN" DESIGNER

By the early 1970s, Calvin Klein had already made such an impression on the fashion industry that he was becoming a fashion icon. For many, his work was quintessentially "American," which referred to numerous qualities in his designs. First of all, his dresses had both classic silhouettes and classic tailoring; they fit a woman's body naturally and comfortably. Second, his designs were simple and clean, which meant they were minimally detailed and accessorized. Third, Klein loved to use natural fabrics like cotton, wool, linen, flannel, suede, and tweed. Klein loathed synthetic fabrics like polyester and rayon. A design assistant from those years remarked, "All of a sudden, [Klein] stopped using polyester—he stopped being afraid, and it took the sportswear to the next level of being really loose and really beautiful. It was kind of revolutionary." Fourth, Klein's models were all-American looking: tall, athletic, clean-cut, and classically beautiful. Fifth, Klein fully embraced the casual, sporty look that Americans loved. Finally, many of his pieces were instantly recognizable American classics, but with a twist: a peacoat with eight buttons, a large-silhouetted trench coat, or a bathrobe made from printed fabric.

In other ways, Klein was experimenting. He began using his own name as a logo on T-shirts. As his name became more famous—it was slowly becoming a brand—people wanted it printed on their clothing. Also distinctive was Klein's color palette. It was almost always soft and neutral. Subtle shades of brown and cream were the norm; if he went bold, it was with chocolate brown or solid black and white. Klein also designed fashions for women that had a masculine look, only softer.

DESIGNS FOR "REGULAR" WOMEN

By the late 1960s, everyday looks were influencing many of the world's top designers. For Calvin Klein, his interest in clothes worn by "regular" women went all the way back to his trips to Paris with

Ralph Lauren

If Calvin Klein has a rival for the title of "great American designer," it would have to be Ralph Lauren. Klein and Lauren grew up in the same neighborhood of the Bronx. After high school, their careers went in similar directions, but Lauren beat Klein to the game on a number of occasions. He developed a menswear collection in 1968, a full decade and a half before Klein did, and his London flagship store was the first by an American designer to open in Europe. Lauren began in 1967 with a collection of men's neckties; the following year saw the debut of his famous "Polo by Ralph Lauren" menswear collection consisting of preppy sweaters and short-sleeved knit shirts. Today, when someone refers to a "polo shirt," everyone knows exactly what is meant. Lauren's version of the classic American look was largely borrowed from American history; his Polo collection was directly inspired by 1920s American fashion seen on affluent, Ivy League campuses like Princeton University, with a touch of cowboy thrown in. Lauren's passion for athletic wear as well as sportswear has set him apart from other designers. His Polo Sport line includes, for example, both boots for hiking and boots for skiing. In the 1970s, he looked to American history for inspiration again with his "prairie look," a collection of leisurely, understated pieces in natural fabrics like suede. Lauren and Klein were on similar courses in the 1980s during the men's-suits-for-women craze. Lauren's "dress for success" women's suit jacket with outlined edges was a breakthrough piece of the genre. Another similarity between the two is their lasting, far-reaching empires. Today, Ralph Lauren offers sportswear, swimwear, children's clothes, bedroom linens, eyeglasses, and, of course, numerous fragrances. The two original scents, Ralph Lauren for women and Polo for men, remain standards of the industry. Ralph Lauren won the Lifetime Achievement Award from the Council of Fashion Designers of America in 1992. He will be remembered in fashion history alongside Calvin Klein as one of the designers most associated with the leisurely, sporty American lifestyle. "I'm not selling clothes," Lauren has said, "I'm offering a world, a philosophy of life. I stand for a look that is American."

Dan Millstein. While many top designers couldn't imagine designing clothes for women who weren't wealthy or of the upper class, Klein loved it. "I personally like to think that I reach people who have a personal style and who don't wait for *Vogue* to tell them what they should buy," Klein said to *Vogue Hommes International* in 2007. Furthermore, by the early 1970s, there was a whole new class of working women who weren't staying at home and raising children. These women needed professional, stylish clothes, and Klein was the right designer for the job.

Klein's response to the needs of "today's woman" marked a new chapter in his career. He began by breaking away from making mostly coats, suits, and dresses. He instead released collections of separates like pants, sweaters, linen blouses, and flannel skirts, all of which could be worn in different combinations in different settings—to work, to dinner, to a job interview, or to church. His jackets were so loosely styled that they resembled a shirt, and they were so versatile that they could be worn with a skirt or with pants. Some of his separates were rather sporty, too. "[Klein] understood that women wanted clothes that worked for them, not clothes that they had to work at," says fashion writer Jane Mulvagh.

RECOGNIZED BY THE INDUSTRY

In the 1940s, a cosmetics company named Coty, Inc., created an award called the Coty American Fashion Critics' Award (nicknamed the "Winnie") to honor outstanding achievement in fashion design. They awarded designers in the areas of womenswear, menswear, and overall achievement. In 1973, Klein won his first "Winnie" and went on to receive the award the following two years as well. In 1974, his sportswear line was honored, a creative collection of beach wear mixed with soft fabrics, like bikini bottoms with brightly colored cardigan sweaters. Eventually the Coty Awards were discontinued as a more powerful organization took hold of the industry in the 1980s.

THE CFDA

The Council of Fashion Designers of America (CFDA) is the most influential organization in the American fashion industry today. Founded in 1962 by a group of fashion designers, the CFDA spends time and money supporting outstanding new designers. The council also recognizes established designers with annual awards. Calvin Klein won the CFDA's prestigious "Best American Collection" award in 1987. In 1993, he won both Menswear Designer of the Year and Womenswear Designer of the Year. In 2001, he was honored with the Lifetime Achievement award. Even though Klein has in recent years reduced his daily role at Calvin Klein, Inc., his successors continue to impress the CFDA. His chief womenswear designer, Francisco Costa, won Womenswear Designer of the year in 2006 and 2008.

KLEIN'S MODELS

At his sportswear runway show in 1974, Klein introduced another of his signatures: thin, sexy models showing a lot of bare skin. In fact, a few of his female models were not wearing underwear under their cardigans, and the flash of skin caused a scandal in the fashion press. Soon his provocative presentation would get him in the middle of controversy, but for the moment, he was making a huge splash. Sex was selling: Women bought his clothes because they felt more attractive when they wore them.

FAMILY CHANGES

Klein's rapid rise was affecting his marriage. Jayne was having difficulty dealing with Klein's absence from both their marriage and the raising of their daughter, Marci. There seemed to be no solution other than to begin divorce proceedings. Unfortunately, the divorce was contentious and ugly. Jayne felt that she deserved a large sum of money so that she and Marci would be comfortable. Klein, who worshipped his little girl, was also concerned with Marci's welfare. The divorce was completed in the summer of 1974.

Calvin Klein is applauded at the end of his 1978 Fall/Winter show.

Interestingly, friends of the couple saw an actual improvement in their relationship in the years that followed; sometimes Jayne was present at Klein's fashion shows and they always spoke politely to each other. Jayne was also receiving generous monetary support from Klein, which he never challenged or minded. He just cared that most of the money was going toward his beloved Marci.

Newly single, Klein moved into a large, luxurious apartment on New York's East Side. The apartment building was exclusive and seemed suited to Klein's new social status and ever-growing wealth. His friends noticed that as he became more wealthy and successful, he also became more private.

Around this time, Klein was enjoying his fame and living a fast-paced lifestyle. Most of his friends were rich and famous, and they spent a lot of time partying at exclusive nightclubs like Studio 54 in New York. He and his friends were so rich they could just fly to the Caribbean for the weekend and be back in New York by Monday morning to go to work. Unfortunately, this frantic lifestyle was not completely healthy for Klein. He began to experiment with drugs and was soon getting little sleep as he partied the nights away, sometimes after a full day at work.

LICENSING

As his business expanded, Klein realized that he did not want to spend long hours and vast sums of money manufacturing every item in his ever-growing collection. In other words, Klein did not want to become a manufacturer-designer like his old boss Dan Millstein. So Klein and Schwartz decided to allow others to use the Calvin Klein name on their products for a fee, called a royalty. This practice, called licensing, is common today, but at the time it was a somewhat novel idea, especially for a fashion designer. When a company licenses its name or image to another company, both parties benefit. The manufacturer, or licensee, makes money because the licensor's name (e.g., "Calvin Klein") is so famous. In turn, the licensor collects a healthy royalty as it becomes more broadly known as a brand.

In his licensing agreements, Klein always insisted on creative control of the products that bore his name. He very well understood the importance of consistency. For example, any accessories with "Calvin Klein" printed on them had to be of the same quality and style of his main line of clothing or else the brand name would be weakened. "Calvin Klein" always had to stand for quality.

Licensing soon became a profitable part of the company. Among their licensees was a famous furrier named Alixandre, who produced Klein's line of furs and fur-lined coats. Alixandre also designed a new version of the peacoat for Klein. Other licenses were for belts by a Canadian company named Omega and umbrellas by Mespo. With the expense of manufacturing the clothes taken off their shoulders, the two men reaped the benefits in the form of royalties and additional licensing fees. Led by strong sales and boosted by licensing, business for Calvin Klein, Ltd., was booming. In 1974, the company earned more than $17 million—a staggering sum in those days and a large increase from the previous year.

With the success of his business, Klein became more of a fixture on New York City's nightlife scene. Here, he is pictured with Frances Stein (*left*), Giorgio Saint Angelo (*second from right*), and an unidentified guest in 1978. A former *Vogue* editor, Stein became an important member of Klein's creative team.

IN THE OFFICE

One of the main reasons Calvin Klein, Ltd., was such a success in the early days was that Barry Schwartz ran a tight ship. Schwartz was strict with the finances and the employees. To some, it seemed that neither man trusted anyone except the other. Schwartz, who had unhappy memories of his years running the family grocery store, was determined to do it his way. Klein had significant input but remained somewhat aloof. He let Schwartz handle almost every aspect of the business, which grew to employ many people, including designers, patternmakers, assistants, tailors, and accountants.

Around this time, Klein also began working with a woman named Frances Stein. Stein, a tough, opinionated woman whose fine taste Klein trusted without exception, used to work as an editor at *Vogue* magazine. Many in the company felt she was as important to Klein creatively as Schwartz was to him business-wise. She had an impeccable eye for putting together an outfit out of seemingly nothing. She was, in a word, a perfectionist, just like Klein. And like Schwartz, she had a bad temper. Her tantrums were almost as legendary as Schwartz's, neither of which helped the general atmosphere at the office.

NEW IDEAS

Soon Klein and Schwartz began a new practice of carefully selecting which stores could carry and display their clothes. Their goal was to give Klein a touch of exclusivity while maintaining the clothes' accessibility to everyday women. In other words, the clothes could be bought at department stores, but only the very best ones like Bloomingdale's and Bergdorf Goodman. Interestingly, as the business grew, Schwartz was actually reducing the number of stores around the country that sold Calvin Klein clothes. The partners wanted the brand to seem special and rarified.

Another new idea was to install mini-Calvin Klein boutiques inside certain department stores—a common practice now but an

---

ELEMENTS OF STYLE

On one occasion, [a fashion critic for] the Chicago Daily News *was just plain rude. [In her review] she didn't talk about the clothes. She talked about me, which I think is terribly unfair. It was a nasty personal attack, and that's not what the press is invited to do when I show my work. I don't mind the clothes' being criticized, but I'm not on the runway! We did this show at a new club called the Flamingo, and we didn't police it properly. People came to crash the show, there weren't enough ushers seating everyone and a couple of fights broke out.*

Calvin Klein in Playboy *magazine*

innovative concept in the 1970s. In 1975, the first Calvin Klein in-store boutique opened inside Bloomingdale's in New York. The opening-night party was a major event and included a fashion show. What the invited guests saw was something very different from what they were used to from Klein. Not only were there more colors than usual, but the colors were vibrant. The show was a hit, and everyone loved the new designs.

A Big Event

One of the most important events in the early years of Klein's career was his fashion show in the fall of 1975. For its setting, Klein chose a trendy New York nightclub, an unheard of practice in those days. Klein wanted more than a fashion show; he wanted to stage an "event." The show would be more like a theatrical production than a fashion show, and he spared no expense with the lights and sound. He ordered an astounding 1,500 sample pieces, eventually selecting about 350 to show on the runway—still a huge number. Extravagant runway shows are common now, but they weren't done back then. Klein once again was ahead of his time.

The night of the show, the fashions were an extraordinary hit, but the show itself was a flop. The biggest problem was that the nightclub was much too small to accommodate all the attendees. Many important members of the fashion industry were refused entry to the show, and others walked out in sheer frustration at not being able to find a seat with a view of the runway. For the first time, Klein drew some bad press.

However, the negative reaction to this notorious show didn't hurt sales; if anything, it enhanced Klein's reputation as a cutting-edge leader in the industry. Not only did he win his third consecutive Coty award that year, but he was inducted into the Coty Hall of Fame for fashion designers. Klein was only 33 years old, the youngest designer ever so honored. Never one to disappoint, Klein designed another fantastic new collection of clothes to be shown at his Hall of Fame induction ceremony.

6

New Directions

By the late 1970s, Klein was a celebrity and a household name. For millions of women, his name was a trusted brand that meant style and quality. At the end of 1977, the company's annual sales reached an astonishing $90 million. He had conquered women's clothes and was ready to expand to other areas. Three important new collections were going to debut in the coming year: fragrances and cosmetics, menswear, and blue jeans. Klein was riding high. But first he had to survive an unexpected and horrible event in early 1978.

KIDNAPPING

Early in the morning on February 3, 1978, Klein was still asleep in bed. The previous evening, he had gone to bed with an upset stomach. Klein lived alone. Since his and Jayne's divorce, their 11-year-old daughter, Marci, had been living with her mother, though Klein saw her most weekends.

Klein was awakened by the sound of the telephone ringing. On the other end of the line was a man who spoke with a foreign accent. The man told Klein that he had kidnapped Marci and would only release her if Klein handed over $100,000. Klein refused to believe it until he heard his daughter's terrified voice on the line. Klein knew then that the nightmare was true: Marci was being held for ransom. In an instant, Klein decided he would do anything and everything possible to get her back. His mind was racing as he hung up the phone. Wasn't Marci staying at Jayne's apartment? She was, but Jayne was out of town. But Marci was being watched by babysitters, wasn't she? Where were her babysitters? The first person he called was Barry Schwartz. His best friend was horrified and suggested Klein call their lawyer. Their lawyer, in turn, promised to call the police and the FBI.

Two Desperate People

The story behind the kidnapping was one of desperation. That morning, Marci got on a bus to go to school and was met by one of her babysitters. Marci was a little surprised, for it was not the woman watching her while her mom was away but another babysitter who worked only when the regular sitter was unavailable. The woman, Christine Ransay, chatted with Marci as they sat on the bus. Christine told Marci that her father was very sick and that they needed to go to a hospital. Frightened by this news, Marci agreed. They got off the bus and got in a taxicab. Marci thought they were going to a hospital, but instead, they went to a dangerous neighborhood. They entered an apartment building where Marci expected to see her dad. Instead, she was tied up and gagged. She met her main kidnapper, Christine's half brother, Dominique Ransay. Dominique then called Klein at home.

Dominique and Christine Ransay were originally from the island of Martinique in the Caribbean Sea, which accounted for their accents. They had been raised in New York, however. Christine Ransay knew the Klein family, because she worked as a waitress at a restaurant owned by Jayne Klein's new boyfriend. She got to know Jayne and became an occasional babysitter for Marci. Both she and her half brother were struggling financially. So Dominique hatched a plan: They would kidnap Marci and refuse to give her up until they were paid a lot of money. Dominique had a criminal record and had spent time in jail.

Dominique had begun planning the kidnapping months earlier. To prepare, he learned everything he could about Calvin Klein. He went to Klein's apartment and office, secretly took pictures of him, and recorded how he lived and behaved. It was as if he were researching a biography. He also followed little Marci, making sure he knew her route to and from school. After some months, he felt ready to go. He was sure he had thought of everything.

Rescuing Marci Klein

While Klein's lawyer called the FBI, Schwartz went to their bank to withdraw the $100,000 in cash. When the two FBI agents arrived, they sprayed the bills with a chemical that would record the kidnappers' fingerprints. Dominique called Klein again to tell him where to drop off the money. The FBI was listening in on the call and was able to trace it to the mysterious apartment building. Klein, fearing for Marci's safety, insisted on going through with the delivery of the ransom money.

A complicated set of instructions from Dominique led Klein to the famous Pan Am Building on Manhattan's East Side. As instructed, Klein dropped an envelope filled with money at a designated spot. Dominique was certain he had pulled it off. He grabbed the envelope and called Klein a final time to tell him where to find Marci. When Klein arrived at the apartment, he found his little girl sitting quietly with Christine, both of them

Calvin Klein leads his daughter, Marci, away from the apartment where kidnappers held her for ransom.

looking frightened. Klein instantly grabbed Marci and hugged her tight for a few seconds before racing out of the apartment. The FBI was already there, ready to grab Christine as soon as they saw that Marci was safe. Christine was promptly arrested for kidnapping.

Because he was her half brother, Dominique was brought in for questioning by the FBI. Eventually, Christine and Dominique confessed to the crime. Dominique offered Klein a weak apology, but for Klein, the ordeal was over. At their trial later that fall, the Ransays pleaded guilty and each received sentences of 25 years, the maximum punishment for second-degree kidnapping.

The ordeal of Marci's kidnapping greatly disturbed Klein. In the months that followed, he saw more of her than usual, and he and Jayne got along better. They wanted Marci to feel like the family was united behind her, even though they were divorced. Klein said later that it was Marci who helped him recover from the experience: "[Marci] helped me understand that life goes on. We had a very touching phone conversation about two weeks after the kidnapping, and she said, 'I just want you to think about not being frightened, about the fact that I'm okay, that we're all okay. I've got schoolwork to do, you've got to design clothes, so let's try to live as normal a life as possible.'" Once he was sure Marci was recovering from the trauma, he turned his attention to the launch of three new collections, each of which represented a new frontier for Klein.

FRAGRANCE AND COSMETICS

Klein had yet to enter a lucrative area of the fashion world: perfume. Almost all the most famous designers in the world had their own signature scent, the most famous being Coco Chanel's Chanel No. 5. After the success of his womenswear, Klein was considering entering the fragrance market as well. One of the attractions of the fragrance business was that big money could be made: Perfume was cheap to make and could be sold at a high price. Further, because perfume was regarded as a luxury item, women were willing to pay more for perfume than the clothes in their daily wardrobe. It seemed to be an ideal moment for Klein to get in on the game; by this time, it seemed like every fashion-conscious woman wanted a Calvin Klein product of some kind. A middle-class woman who couldn't afford an expensive Calvin Klein dress might be able to afford a bottle of Calvin Klein perfume.

Though potentially there was a lot of money to be made, starting a fragrance line was extremely costly. For one thing, consumers tended to tire of perfumes quickly, so the initial advertising campaign for a new fragrance had to be elaborate. Such a campaign could cost tens of millions of dollars. At first, Klein considered licensing his name to a big cosmetics company like Revlon, but, as usual, he wanted control of every aspect of the product (and Schwartz wanted all the profits). So Calvin Klein Cosmetics was born.

In addition to perfume, Calvin Klein Cosmetics would, of course, offer cosmetics. For this new line of makeup products, Klein, who was famous for neutral colors, had to embrace vivid colors like reds and pinks, or the items wouldn't sell. To run this new wing of the company, Klein and Schwarz lured a man named Stanley Kohlenberg away from Revlon.

The first and most important decision Klein and his fragrance team had to make was the selection of the scent. It was a decision that divided the company. Klein and Frances Stein were partial to a scent that Stein discovered in Paris, but Kohlenberg was enthusiastic about a fragrance developed by a company that specialized in creating scents. Because Klein was new to the business, this latter company was the safer choice, Kohlenberg felt. Furthermore, the fragrance that Klein and Stein preferred would be very expensive to recreate.

Klein, however, went with his gut and ordered Kohlenberg to copy the floral-scented perfume that he and Stein favored. Reluctantly, Kohlenberg did so. Adding to the pressure, Ralph Lauren had just scored a big win with his massively successful Polo cologne for men and Lauren perfume for women. Also, the Ralph Lauren scents were offered at Bloomingdale's— Klein's home for many years. Klein and Schwartz were forced to approach another department store, Saks Fifth Avenue, for their fragrance launch.

An Unexpected Flop

The fragrance, simply named Calvin Klein, appeared in stores in February 1978. It was a complete and utter flop. It was a significant moment—Calvin Klein's first real business failure. Schwartz, ever the businessman, reacted severely. He abruptly shut down Calvin Klein Cosmetics in late 1979. It is estimated that Klein and Schwartz lost about $4 million in their fragrance venture.

Closing down Calvin Klein Cosmetics was not to be the end of the story, however. Shortly after the cosmetics line closed, a company named Minnetonka Industries approached Klein. The owner, Robert Taylor, wanted to buy the Calvin Klein Cosmetics label. As the licensee, Taylor would have permission to use the Calvin Klein name to sell new fragrances that he would manufacture and sell. Klein, as the licensor, would retain control of the product and its branding and collect a hefty royalty. After difficult negotiations, a deal was reached. Minnetonka would prepare a new and improved line of Calvin Klein fragrances and cosmetics.

DESIGNING FOR MEN

Stung by the failure of Calvin Klein Cosmetics, Klein and Schwartz turned their attention to an area of the industry that seemed more fruitful. Considering the success of his women's line, it was only logical that Klein would eventually develop a line of clothes for men.

Menswear in the Twentieth Century

The history of American menswear is similar to that of womenswear in that both were influenced by sportswear. For many decades, American men were accustomed to wearing suits, shirts, and ties to every occasion unless they were playing sports. As the years passed, athletic clothes made their way into men's daily wear. Its appeal was the same as it was for women: Sportswear was more comfortable and less expensive than formal wear. Today, sportswear is everywhere, and men typically wear suits only to formal occasions and to work—and even at work it is becoming less

After he experienced success with his womenswear, Klein challenged himself by debuting a menswear line. Here, he poses before a show in 1979.

common. Designers like Ralph Lauren, Geoffrey Beene, and Perry Ellis paved the way with their men's collections in the 1970s, all heavily influenced by sportswear.

An Enormous Collection

When Klein announced his plan, the industry was startled. Klein was planning to go big right from the start: His menswear collection would include every imaginable piece of a man's wardrobe—shirts, pants, suits, sweaters, belts, socks, and underwear. Of course, the biggest challenge was the same as with the fragrance line: He needed an enormous amount of money to launch it. In fact, the launch of the menswear line was going to cost even more than the fragrance line.

Faced with this, Klein and Schwartz did what was becoming second nature for them: They searched for a licensee to foot the bill. The two men felt they would not have to look very long or very hard; a Calvin Klein fragrance and cosmetics line might seem like a gamble, but clothes were what Klein was known for and what he did well. Almost on cue, a man named Maurice Bidermann came forward. Bidermann was the head of a huge manufacturing empire that could easily handle the cost, which was estimated at $30 million. Soon a licensing deal was made for Bidermann's company to manufacture a new Calvin Klein Menswear line, with Klein earning a healthy 7 percent royalty.

Klein's menswear line was cut for "American builds"—the idea being that American men are stockier and more broad-shouldered than European men. The collection of men's sweaters, pants, shirts, and suits that premiered in early 1978 consisted of thousands of pieces made from some 800 different fabrics. It was by any measure an enormous collection, and it was extremely successful. Klein had gambled again, and this time he won. He had jumped into the menswear world feet first and rose to the top. Calvin Klein Menswear would make $40 million in its first year.

JEANS

Originally manufactured in the 1850s for gold miners in San Francisco, denim blue jeans were typically worn by farmers and working-class people. By the late 1960s, however, more fashionable versions of blue jeans began to appear. For example, bell-bottom jeans were popular with young students on college campuses. Bell-bottoms were just the beginning of the surge in popularity

Blue Jeans

Though his first attempt was unsuccessful, it makes perfect sense that a classic American designer like Calvin Klein should find success selling one of the great American clothing fixtures: blue jeans. The history of blue jeans begins with a man named Levi Strauss. Originally from Germany, Strauss came to the United States in 1850 during the San Francisco Gold Rush. Mining was hard, dirty work, and Strauss noticed that many miners didn't have sturdy pants that could stand up to repeated wear and tear. He first hired a tailor to make pants from canvas but soon changed to denim. Denim is a durable cotton twill fabric that is dyed blue. ("Twill" means that the threads of cotton are woven diagonally.) Denim blue jeans' popularity as work clothes grew quickly. Soon everyone from farmers and cowboys to factory workers were wearing jeans and overalls made by companies like Levi's, Lee, and Wrangler. During World War II, soldiers took their blue jeans with them overseas, spreading their popularity to Europe and Asia. In the 1950s, blue jeans were equally popular with high school kids and their parents. By the 1960s, European and American fashion designers began to create leisure clothes made of denim to go along with traditional blue jeans. A pair of blue jeans was an essential part of every person's wardrobe by the 1970s and 1980s, and today you can buy just about every kind of blue jean imaginable—dyed, bleached, faded, boot cut, stonewashed, skinny, and slim fitting. Some blue jeans aren't even blue! Blue jeans show no sign of losing their status as America's greatest contribution to casual fashion. Yves Saint Laurent put it best when he said, "I have often said that I wish I had invented blue jeans: the most spectacular, the most practical, the most relaxed and nonchalant. They have expression, modesty, sex appeal, simplicity."

experienced by blue jeans. It took a wealthy New York socialite named Gloria Vanderbilt to erase blue jeans' working-class reputation and turn them into a high-fashion item.

Gloria Vanderbilt

Gloria Vanderbilt was a member of the rich and famous Vanderbilt family, which had earned its wealth in the railroad industry. Trained as a visual artist, Vanderbilt launched a line of designer blue jeans in 1976. Tight fitting and expensive, Vanderbilt jeans were immediately recognizable by their rear end: The Vanderbilt name was sewn on the back pocket. In her fifties but still curvaceous and attractive, Gloria Vanderbilt was not really a designer (she was essentially licensing her famous name), but it didn't matter; her jeans caused the designer jeans market to explode. Everyone, it seemed, wanted a pair of designer jeans. Soon other famous designers began manufacturing their own line of jeans, including Calvin Klein, who tried his own line that same year. It was not a successful venture. Not only did people complain that his jeans

Gloria Vanderbilt poses among models showing off her namesake jeans. Vanderbilt took the utilitarian blue jean and dressed it up, opening the door for designers like Calvin Klein to offer a range of designer blue jeans.

ELEMENTS OF STYLE

In 1977, I was at Studio 54, dancing, at four A.M. I was going to Frankfurt [Germany] the next day and decided to stay up all night, then get on the plane and sleep. A guy from Puritan came up to me and asked if I would be interested in putting my name on jeans. "I could guarantee you at least $1 million a year," he told me. . . . I straightened myself real quickly, because when someone talks business, I listen. . . . His offer would give me an opportunity to reach many people. . . . I thought it could be a fun thing to do.

Calvin Klein in Playboy *magazine*

didn't fit well, but they were more expensive than Vanderbilt's. Klein quickly dropped the line and swore never to be in the jeans business again.

They would prove to be famous last words, for just a few years later, Klein was approached with the idea of licensing the Calvin Klein name for a new line of blue jeans. Puritan Fashions was a large garment company known for its extremely cheap (and, some felt, tasteless) dresses sold at discount department stores. Puritan's owner, Carl Rosen, wanted to move into a higher-end part of the industry, and Calvin Klein was an ideal potential partner. When Rosen approached Klein, however, Puritan was in decline. It had lost the business of the new class of working women who wanted (and could afford) fashionable, ready-to-wear outfits made by designers like Calvin Klein.

While Rosen appeared to need Klein more than Klein needed him, a licensing deal with Puritan would be a good move for Klein, too. First of all, Rosen had a reputation for knowing how to manufacture women's clothes, and he had made an enormous fortune doing so. If anyone could successfully mass-produce a line of blue jeans, it was Rosen. Secondly, Rosen was no stranger to licensing; he owned the license for the image of the Beatles. That, too, had earned Rosen millions. Klein and Schwartz began negotiations with Rosen, and soon the men had a deal. Rosen offered $1 million up front for use of the Calvin Klein name as well as $1 million every year thereafter. For his part, Klein insisted on what was always most important to him: creative control. Klein would oversee the jeans' design as well as the images used in advertising.

Calvin Klein Jeans

The jeans themselves were high waisted, straight legged, and tight fitting. Klein said, "The tighter they are, the better they sell." A pair cost about $40 and could be found wherever other Calvin Klein clothes were sold. Barry Schwartz thought they might sell about a million pairs in their first year.

Schwartz was wrong—in a big way. A stupefying 200,000 pairs were sold in just the *first week*, and within a year, Calvin Klein jeans were second only to Gloria Vanderbilt's in sales. Puritan Fashions earned $80 million in total sales in 1978, and a full third of that amount was derived from sales of Calvin Klein jeans. The designer would add men's jeans to the line in 1979, boosting profits even further. Klein had entered a new area of the fashion industry, and once again, had hit a home run.

THE END OF A CHALLENGING YEAR

The year 1978 had proved to be a remarkable, if challenging, year for Klein. It began with the horror of his daughter's kidnapping, followed by his first major business failure, and ended with him rebounding mightily: Minnetonka's new and improved Calvin Klein perfume had earned $2 million in its first six weeks, the menswear line was an instant hit, and his jeans were selling at an astonishing rate. Most fashion historians point to the late 1970s as Klein's greatest and most successful period.

7

The Image Master

As the 1980s began, Klein was flying high. The licenses for menswear, fragrances, and jeans were all doing extraordinarily well, and he and Schwartz still owned their signature women's line. Klein was rich beyond his wildest dreams, and he was also famous. He was invited to the most exclusive parties and nightclubs on both coasts and regularly appeared in celebrity magazines. As far as his status in the fashion industry was concerned, Klein had outpaced Ralph Lauren and was now the undisputed "great American designer" of his generation. Where he still had room to grow, however, was on the marketing and branding side of the business. In the coming decade, he would become a master of these areas.

Klein understood something very important: In the public's mind, the advertising for a product and the product itself were practically the same thing. The more iconic the advertising, the stronger the brand, and the stronger the brand, the stronger the sales. Klein's goal was to come up with an iconic, high-impact advertising campaign that would make the Calvin Klein brand even more famous than it already was. Klein was about to embark on an extraordinary run as a master creator of branding and image.

A BREAKTHROUGH CAMPAIGN

Calvin Klein's first attempt at establishing his brand occurred in 1978 when the company purchased ad space on a large billboard near busy Times Square in New York City. The ad was for his blue jeans, which were just getting started but were already popular. In the ad, a beautiful woman is kneeling on all fours and throwing her head back so that her blond hair is flying all around her. The dynamic and sexy ad became an instant classic of print advertising. Suddenly, not only was the fashion press talking about Klein, but the advertising world was taking notice as well. Furthermore, the ad had its intended effect: Sales of Calvin Klein jeans went through the roof.

ELEMENTS OF STYLE

I drive down Broadway every day to my studio, and I purposely have the Calvin Klein billboards arranged in Times Square so that I can see them. I originally had one billboard that faced downtown, and it upset me terribly, because I would have to turn back and look back through the rear window to see it. So I decided to take two billboards: one facing north—so that as I'm driving south, I can see it in front of me—and the second one facing south, which I turn around to see. But believe me, I don't think about my fame very much and I don't dwell on success. Maybe that's one reason I'm successful. It's always the new challenge that keeps me interested.

Calvin Klein in Playboy *magazine*

Brooke Shields

After witnessing the media frenzy surrounding their first billboard, Klein and Schwartz were anxious to follow it up with an even bigger splash. Klein's friend, the famous fashion photographer Richard Avedon, had recently finished a photo shoot for *Vogue* featuring a 15-year-old model and actress named Brooke Shields. One afternoon, Avedon was showing the photos to Klein, and Klein was immediately impressed. Her youth and beauty were exactly what he was looking for. He selected Shields as his next model for Calvin Klein jeans.

For this ad campaign, Klein did something different. Not only were there going to be print ads in magazines, but Klein wanted to make television commercials as well. Avedon got to work creating commercials that would revolutionize television advertising. He shot 12 different ads all featuring young Brooke Shields in various poses and outfits against a pure white background. Not only were the images instantly iconic, but Klein's copywriters created tag lines that were just as memorable. In one ad, Shields utters the now-famous line, "Do you know what comes between me and my Calvins? Nothing." What's particularly clever is that the jeans are not referred to as "jeans" but as "Calvins." This is exactly what Klein hoped to achieve. In the ad, the brand ("my Calvins") is synonymous with the product itself (the jeans). It was a masterpiece of both branding and copywriting. When added to Avedon's compelling imagery, it was an instant hit.

The commercials began running in August 1980, and they were an immediate sensation. Shields became famous, and sales of Calvin Klein jeans soared; 400,000 pairs sold in just the first week after the TV ads began running, and eventually they reached sales of 2 million pairs a month.

Controversy

In the fall of 1980, television stations began airing a new set of six Calvin Klein jeans commercials. Once again, Brooke Shields was featured, but this set of ads was even more sexually suggestive than

Klein stands with Brooke Shields in a DJ booth at Studio 54 in 1981. As a young model, Shields starred in an ad campaign for Calvin Klein jeans, famously saying, "Do you know what comes between me and my Calvins? Nothing."

the last. They created another sensation, but this time controversy came with it. Television stations that ran the ads began receiving phone calls complaining that the ads were simply too racy; some even considered them obscene. What seemed to bother people the most was Shields's age; she was clearly younger than 18 and yet she was behaving in an adult manner. The protests intensified, and some callers asked television stations to take the ads off the air completely. Many stations—including some in big cities like New York and Los Angeles—gave in to the pressure and stopped airing the ads.

Klein mounted a vigorous defense. "People said we were taking advantage of a fifteen-year-old, which was not the truth," Klein explained a few years later. "We were using Brooke as an actress; she was playing different roles; a liberated woman, a teenager . . . the intention was to do something that was interesting and different." Even in 2007, he was still defending himself: "I never tried to be gratuitously provocative. . . . I simply wanted to create a strong image and sell a product."

For his next set of jeans ads, Klein asked Avedon to tone it down. These new ads featured a group of women laughing and talking about their lives. Devoid of any sexual content, the ads were a breakthrough of another sort: There was no mention of blue jeans at all. The ad seemed to say that their Calvin Klein jeans were so much a part of these women's lives that the women didn't have to even mention them. Klein explained this masterpiece of subtle advertising: "There is no way to advertise jeans today by trying to push the jeans and make *them* interesting; it's been done. The only way to advertise is by not focusing on the product . . . my attitude is 'If you want to sell jeans, don't talk about them.'"

MEN'S UNDERWEAR

While enjoying the success of his blue jeans line, Klein made plans to launch a line for which he would become well known: men's underwear. Klein saw it as a natural extension of his men's collection: "A designer who designs for men should do everything for men."

However, Klein already had competition. He had been beaten to the fashion underwear game by the Jockey corporation, which in 1981 had started a line of stylish men's underwear. The trend of using a celebrity as a model had caught on, and so Jockey asked Jim Palmer, a pitcher for the Baltimore Orioles baseball team, to represent Jockey underwear. Palmer was well known to millions of American men, and sales for Jockey underwear took off. Jockey had achieved an important branding success: Just as Calvin Klein jeans were called "Calvins," a man's briefs were his "Jockeys" or "Jockey shorts." Jockey was dominating the market, and Klein had his work cut out for him if he was going to elbow his way into the men's underwear industry.

Maurice Bidermann, who was still producing the rest of Klein's massive menswear line, manufactured the first collection of Calvin

Klein underwear. It consisted of traditional white briefs, boxer shorts, white undershirts, and bikini-style briefs. A three-pack of Calvin Klein white briefs cost $14.50, which was rather expensive in those days, but it didn't matter. By then, the Calvin Klein brand was so strongly associated with style, quality, and sexiness that even the simple briefs sold extremely well. Klein also made strides toward his branding goal by stitching the name "Calvin Klein" into the elastic waistband of every pair of briefs. When a man changed his clothes at the gym, or if his jeans rode a little low on his waist one day, everyone would see that he was wearing Calvin Klein underwear.

The Campaign

For the advertising, Klein needed to do something bold if he was going to compete with Jockey's Jim Palmer ads. In his ads, Klein wanted to acknowledge openly and boldly that underwear made many people think of sex, so he commissioned a set of provocative photos from photographer Bruce Weber. Weber was known for his sensuous photographs of muscular, barely clothed male models. In addition to their sexual appeal, Weber's models had a natural, all-American look; he often hired college-aged men and professional athletes. It was exactly the image Klein was going for: a sexy "boy next door."

The first Calvin Klein men's underwear model was an Olympic pole-vaulter named Tom Hintnaus. When it first appeared in the fall of 1983, the Times Square billboard of Hintnaus wearing only his underwear created a sensation. The ad was photographed in a Mediterranean location and featured Hintnaus holding a discus. Weber was clearly conjuring the image of a Greek god.

New Controversy

Not everyone loved the image, however. Just as with the Brooke Shields jeans ads, the Hintnaus ad was met with a chorus of outrage. This time, Klein didn't care; he ordered large-sized prints of the ads to appear in New York bus stop shelters. Soon there were reports of

A billboard for Calvin Klein underwear overlooks New York City's Times Square in 1983. The campaign starred Olympic pole-vaulter Tom Hintnaus and was responsible for a spike in sales.

people breaking the glass and stealing the posters for themselves. The ad campaign worked: Not only were men buying the underwear, but their girlfriends and wives were buying it for them.

Sales for men's underwear were incredible: $4 million in just the first year. Klein expanded the line to include different styles like boxer briefs and trunk-style briefs. He also offered an array of colors from bright red to oatmeal. So successful was the men's underwear line that Klein soon released a line of women's underwear, accompanied by yet another sexy ad campaign. The underwear side of the company grew so fast (earning $70 million in 1984, for example) that Klein and Schwartz sold off the women's side to a licensee. Klein, as always, retained control of the line's design and image. Just as he had done so many times before, Klein successfully moved into an area of the fashion industry and made it his own.

CHANGES IN MENSWEAR AND JEANS

As the men's underwear line took off, it appeared to do so at the expense of the regular menswear collection, which was seeing a significant decline in sales. Klein was suspicious that Maurice Bidermann, who owned the licenses for both menswear and men's underwear, was having the menswear made with cheap fabrics and stitching. Klein, ever conscious of his brand, insisted on high quality for all his lines. He insisted that Bidermann improve the quality (and raise the prices) of the menswear. Bidermann resisted, and the two men fought repeatedly. In the end, they could not agree on a single vision for the menswear line, and the long-standing licensing agreement was ended when Klein bought both men's lines back from Bidermann. Now Klein could start a menswear line that would be his and his alone, but it would take time. For a number of years in the late 1980s, there were no men's clothes to be found with the Calvin Klein label on them other than underwear.

Puritan, the company that owned the license for Calvin Klein jeans, was undergoing major changes that would affect the future of one of Klein's most important lines. The man at the head of Puritan, Carl Rosen, was dying of cancer; after an unsuccessful attempt to hand the company over to a new president, Rosen decided to name his 26-year-old son as his successor. Klein and Schwartz were outraged. They could not accept an arrangement

Classic Collaborators

Calvin Klein's phenomenal success in the 1980s owes a great deal to two important collaborators, Richard Avedon and Bruce Weber. A native New Yorker like Klein, Avedon was born in 1923 and is one of the most influential American photographers of his generation and perhaps the most important fashion photographer of all time. His talents were noticed early on, and he landed a staff photographer job at *Harper's Bazaar* in 1945 before moving to *Vogue* in 1966, where he would remain until 1990. His early photographs were active and full of good humor: The women in the photographs seemed to feel great wearing their fashions. As the years went on, Avedon's style changed to something more realistic and serene—even static—yet full of subtle human activity; his subjects came alive on the page. For Klein, however, he was a commercial director, yet even in motion pictures, his sparse, black-and-white style is evident. Avedon died in 2004. Bruce Weber is from a different generation than Avedon's, but he has achieved a similar level of acclaim in the world of fashion photography. Born in Pennsylvania in 1949, Weber's photographs of Olympic pole-vaulter Tom Hintnaus for Calvin Klein underwear put him on the map. Like Avedon's later work, Weber's photography is mostly in black-and-white. Inspired by classical Greek sculpture, Weber became famous for photographing all-American, athletic, nearly nude male models. In addition to his work for Calvin Klein, he has also photographed for Ralph Lauren, Versace, and Abercrombie & Fitch. Today, Weber remains one of the most sought-after fashion photographers in the world.

in which such an inexperienced person would be in charge of their most important and successful clothing line. Furthermore, because of the details of the licensing agreement, Calvin Klein jeans were making more money for Puritan than for Klein and Schwartz; Calvin Klein jeans made up 94 percent of Puritan's annual sales. Klein and Schwartz naturally wanted to own their most profitable item, so they plotted to buy Puritan, eventually succeeding in November 1983. Klein and Schwartz renamed the company Calvin Klein Sport and developed a new line of casual wear for men and women, an area of the business that was growing in popularity.

Menswear Tailoring for Women

A discussion of 1980s-era menswear would not be complete without mentioning the influence that menswear had on the womenswear of the era—in particular on the so-called women's "power suit." Klein and other designers like Gianni Versace and Giorgio Armani dressed women in suits that had the same shape and tailoring as men's suits but were made with softer fabrics such as cashmere. The suits were usually patterned with plaids, tweeds, or checks. The whole look was completed with neckties and suspenders. Ralph Lauren was the champion of women's suit blazers, whose lapels and pockets were edged, or outlined, in a darker color, something that Klein would soon begin doing as well.

A NEW PARTNER

In 1983, Klein met a special woman who won his heart. Kelly Rector was a young designer who had also attended FIT and had worked as both a receptionist and a design assistant for Ralph Lauren. When she applied for a job with Klein at the tender age of 21, her portfolio wasn't terribly impressive, but Klein liked her as a person. She was bright and attractive and had a deep love of fashion, so he hired her as one of his designers. Klein and Rector developed a warm friendship before beginning their romantic relationship. Klein appreciated her insights and good taste; she loved his fun personality, charm, and ceaseless ambition. Soon people noticed that Rector was influencing Klein's designs. For example, where Klein had always looked to Europe for inspiration, Rector, having spent years working at Ralph Lauren, brought a more traditional American sensibility to the designs. Ralph Lauren's Polo collection was inspired by men playing polo on horseback. Rector, herself a horse lover, brought these ideas and images to Klein, who absorbed them into his collections. Rector's influence on Klein frustrated some of Klein's longtime employees, but Klein was loyal to her and even let her make decisions about which designs would be included in a future collection.

In 1986, Klein and Rector went to Italy and eloped. People reacted differently to the new Mrs. Klein. While his daughter, Marci, was happy for her dad, Klein's mother, Flo, reportedly did not approve of the marriage. Others were enchanted with Klein's young bride, especially because she seemed to be such a good influence on him. In her presence, Klein was less shy, for example. But she remained a controversial presence within the company, and some days the office was quite tense. Eventually, she left the company, but her influence on Klein remained.

Getting Healthy

In the late 1980s, all the wild times Klein spent partying in the 1970s finally caught up to him. Klein entered a rehabilitation center in Minnesota to kick an addiction to prescription drugs and alcohol. Over the years, some of those who worked closely with Klein suspected that he might be abusing controlled substances. His mood swings could be severe, and sometimes he did not appear physically well. Becoming clean and sober seemed to rejuvenate Klein. Not long after leaving rehab, Klein remarked, "I'm in the first year of my second life. I feel reborn. I really am seeing things differently."

Klein married Kelly Rector in 1986. A onetime Calvin Klein employee, Rector was responsible for steering Klein toward an American aesthetic.

NEW FRAGRANCES, NEW SUCCESSES

Even with all the successes he had achieved so far in the 1980s, Klein was still not done. He began thinking about one of the areas of the industry that he had not mastered: fragrances. Klein wanted to start over with a new collection of fragrances for two reasons: The Calvin Klein perfumes that were on the market were selling poorly, and Klein and Schwartz could not stand Robert Taylor, the head of the company that manufactured the fragrances. So Klein and Schwartz replaced Taylor and set to work totally revamping Klein's fragrance line.

Obsession

Other than choosing the new scent, the most important decision was how to advertise it. Klein again turned to the photographer who had made such an impression with his men's underwear ads, Bruce Weber. Weber's print ads for the new fragrance, called Obsession, were another huge sensation. But that was not all: TV commercials were created by the same team that had done the Brooke Shields jeans ads. If the print ads created a sensation, photographer Richard Avedon's television ads set off a virtual revolution in television advertising. To this day, they remain among the most memorable television ads in history.

The dreamlike ads for Obsession were a mix of Avedon's and Klein's color palettes: scenes in black-and-white alternating with sequences in beige, tan, and white. While the visual imagery was certainly distinctive, the dialogue spoken by the actors was off the wall. "She loved me and she's gone," complains a young boy in one of the ads. "She's deep in my blood; the only woman I'll ever love." The woman replies, "Love is child's play once you've known Obsession." Another ad has a man ruminating, "She left, and everything golden went with her. . . . Was it me? Did I somehow drive her away?" The tag lines that came at the end of each ad were even more poetic—even strange: "Between love and madness lies Obsession" or "There are many loves, but only one Obsession."

The ads were so unlike anything that had come before that they were both imitated and ridiculed in equal measure—surely a form of flattery. *Saturday Night Live* famously parodied the ads with their hilarious fake commercials for "Canis," a cologne for dogs, and "Compulsion," a cleaning product from "Calvin Kleen."

More seriously, Klein was exploring two new ideas with the Obsession fragrance. First of all, Klein introduced both a men's and women's version of the same fragrance, another new idea for the time. Secondly, the two scents smelled practically the same; Klein was moving toward a "unisex" cologne, something unheard of in the industry to that point.

The multifaceted ad campaign for Obsession cost many millions of dollars, but it was worth it. The fragrance sold amazingly well in just its first few weeks. Taken together, Klein's company would eventually sell more than $100 million of Obsession colognes and lotions for men and women. Many feel that Obsession is Calvin Klein's most famous product of all time, and that is largely due to the amazing television ads by Richard Avedon.

Eternity

Inspired by the enormous success of Obsession, Klein ordered his team to develop a second scent. This scent, for women, would be more floral than Obsession. Inspired by the themes of love and romance, Klein launched Eternity. Another wide-reaching ad campaign was launched, but this time the ads had a different look. Where Obsession was moody, mysterious, and vaguely sexual, the ads for Eternity featured people relaxing at home with children. The Eternity ads seemed to reflect Klein's own life at the time— newly married and embracing a more domestic life.

Escape

Their third fragrance, called Escape, was an adventure into the unknown. At that time, it was almost unheard of for a designer to have more than two fragrances on the market, but Klein was leading the way (as usual) to what would eventually become an industry norm.

If Eternity was about, in Klein's words, "family, commitment, children, and romance," Escape, Klein said, "goes beyond that." Escape, then, was a mix of Eternity and Obsession: The print ads featured the sexy, "get-away-from-it-all" vibe of Obsession, but the television commercials were more like those of Eternity, with couples at home, enjoying their children. Escape was another hit, selling millions of bottles within weeks of being released.

CONTROVERSIAL AND VISIONARY

By the end of the 1980s, Klein had earned a controversial reputation because of his suggestive jeans and underwear ads. Yet he was smart enough to know that no matter what people's objections were, he had captured something essential about the decade. In his 1984 *Playboy* interview, Klein talked about that: "What I'm going to say may seem pretentious, but 20 or 30 years from now, I believe someone may look at all the commercials I've done and view them as a vignette of the times, a reflection of what people were thinking, the moods of today. A young girl talking about a date or who she should sit next to at the movies; Brooke [Shields] talking about her jeans. . . ." Today, after that many years have passed, it is interesting to see how keen his foresight was. But Klein's reputation for controversy was going to grow even larger in the coming decade.

8

Youth Movement

The 1990s began with Calvin Klein facing something unfamiliar: falling sales. Since purchasing Puritan in 1983 and ending the licensing contract with Maurice Bidermann in 1987, Calvin Klein, Inc., was now responsible for jeans, men's underwear, and menswear. Sales for the first two were poor, and there was no menswear line at all. Adding to the difficulty of the situation, the company was also carrying a large amount of debt. Klein and Schwartz had been forced to borrow millions of dollars in the 1980s to keep up with their expanding collections. In the early 1990s, however, America was going through a recession, people's buying habits were changing, and sales were contracting as a result. By the middle of the decade, there was talk, once unimaginable, that Calvin Klein would have to declare bankruptcy and reorganize.

THE NEW MEN'S UNDERWEAR

Just as Klein was worrying about how he and Schwartz were going to pay their debts, a good friend stepped in. David Geffen had been a friend of Klein's since the early 1970s and was an extraordinarily rich record industry executive. As head of Geffen Records, he produced some of the greatest albums of the 1970s, including those by artists such as Cher, Joni Mitchell, and Elton John. Geffen believed in both Klein's talent and Schwartz's business sense, and with a personal worth of more than $1 billion, he made an offer to buy off all of the company's debt. Klein was overwhelmed by his friend's generosity and greatly relieved. Klein promised to repay the loan, which he eventually did, in 1993.

Marky Mark

Geffen asked for little in return for his loan; however, he did offer some advice. Geffen was familiar with a young rapper from Boston named Mark Wahlberg, who performed under the name Marky Mark. The rap music world was largely dominated by African Americans, yet Marky Mark had a loyal following that crossed racial lines. In addition to his music, Marky Mark was popular because he performed without a shirt and sported a ripped, muscular body. Mark was also well known for dropping his pants during his concerts, and surprise!—he wore Calvin Klein briefs. Geffen saw an opening through which Klein could reach an entire new generation of buyers, and the young rapper from Boston held the key.

Geffen helped Klein negotiate a contract with Mark that made the young star the new face (and body) of Calvin Klein men's underwear. Mark was "the male equivalent of Brooke Shields," claimed the vice president of Bloomingdale's department stores. Not surprisingly, sales for Klein's men's underwear skyrocketed, and Mark became a star. In addition to a print campaign featuring Mark, Klein once again ordered television commercials. The TV ad campaign featured Mark alongside a thin young British model named Kate Moss. Appearing together and both wearing nothing on top, Mark and Moss' sexy ads riveted the public and the industry. Where Mark was streetwise and tough, Moss was innocent, childlike, and angelic. It was a potent combination. More than any of Klein's models before or since, Marky Mark and Kate Moss were synonymous with Calvin Klein.

KATE MOSS

The discovery of Kate Moss ushered in a new and controversial era in female modeling. Moss was extremely thin—*too* thin, many felt—and appeared to be younger than her 18 years. Klein loved her. Just as Marky Mark provided the men's underwear line with an electrifying boost, Kate Moss did likewise as the new face of Obsession perfume. Yet once again, Klein's ads

A billboard of Kate Moss advertising Calvin Klein jeans is posted prominently at Broadway and Houston in New York City. As with previous campaigns, Klein set out to provoke, but he drew more controversy from featuring a model who was considered excessively thin and perhaps too young.

stirred controversy, and the objections were not that different than those from 15 years earlier. Many felt the Obsession ads featuring Moss were using an underage girl posed in sexually suggestive positions to sell perfume.

Klein profited so handsomely from the sales of his men's and women's underwear divisions that he was able to sell them both to a company called the Warnaco Group for an incredible $64 million in 1994. Calvin would insist on retaining creative control of the business, however.

THE NEW MENSWEAR

As the rejuvenated men's underwear collection took off, Klein stepped back and reexamined his entire men's line, which, since the ending of the licensing agreement with Maurice Bidermann, no longer included a formal menswear collection. It just so happened that a top Italian menswear manufacturer named GFT wanted to expand beyond the licenses it already held with designers like Armani and Valentino. One designer that GFT was watching closely was Calvin Klein. If a deal could be made, it would be a perfect fit: Calvin Klein was exactly the sort of American brand that the Italian company desired, and GFT offered the clean, modern, European look that Klein wanted for his new-and-improved menswear line. Negotiations began, and while they were difficult, a deal was reached in 1991 for GFT to manufacture a new Calvin Klein menswear line that Klein, of course, would design and control.

COMPETITION AND CHANGING HABITS

When Klein and Schwartz bought the old Puritan company in 1983, they had renamed it Calvin Klein Sport and launched a new line of casual wear. The collection did not sell well. Though they had high hopes for the line, it never caught on. In 1990, for example, Calvin Klein Sport lost an astonishing $14.2 million. One of the reasons that their casual sportswear line was having trouble was intense competition from new stores like The Gap and Banana

A Special Honor

In 1990, Klein received a special honor when the great modern choreographer Martha Graham asked him to design costumes for a new dance piece of hers set to the "Maple Leaf Rag" composed by Scott Joplin. Graham, then 96, thought Klein's sleek, minimalist style would be an interesting contrast to her passionate choreography. Klein's simple, American designs were a perfect fit for the all-American program. Most of the female dancers in the piece wear traditional leotards and tights, and the men are bare-chested with tights. One woman in a pale blue flowing skirt periodically dances across the stage. In addition to the long skirt this woman wears, Klein designed a top for her with an exposed back that Graham takes full advantage of; the woman twists her body as she crosses the stage, making, from the audience's point of view, a circle out of her skirt. The effect is simple and beautiful, and each appearance of this "circle-skirt woman" marks a new section of the piece. "Maple Leaf Rag" would be Graham's final completed work, as she died just a few months after its premiere. Shortly after Graham's death, a performance was filmed so that both Graham's choreography and Klein's costumes could be remembered for all time.

Republic. These stores offered fashionable casual clothes at affordable prices. Another reason was that some companies were starting to allow casual styles in the workplace. On "casual Fridays," for example, employees were allowed to wear jeans and sport shirts to work instead of shirts and ties.

Shopping Malls

As more and more Americans began buying casual wear, their shopping habits reflected this change. Once upon a time, Americans shopped almost exclusively in department stores, in which they could buy everything—sheets for the bedroom, clothes for the children, pots and pans for the kitchen. By the 1980s, however, the popularity of department stores was fading, and many either went out of business or were bought by larger companies.

Taking the place of department stores were shopping malls: large, indoor spaces filled with specialty stores—shoe stores, clothing stores, sporting goods stores, and so on. Malls were usually anchored by one or two major department stores, but they were losing customers to the specialty stores that could offer greater selections. A department store like Boston Store would certainly sell Calvin Klein clothes (it might even have an in-store boutique), but no matter how special the display, Klein would be competing alongside the clothing of other competitors.

Calvin Klein Stores

Klein, who had made a career of anticipating new trends, realized it was time to open Calvin Klein stores in shopping malls across the country. As always with Klein, what appealed to him was *control.* A Calvin Klein store would sell only his products, and it could sell them all: menswear and womenswear, jeans, casual wear, sportswear, fragrances, accessories, and underwear. Further, the design of the actual store could reflect the Calvin Klein style and brand. The store itself would be one giant branding device. Of course, the idea was not unheard of; on Fifth Avenue in New York City, stores devoted to one designer were common. But in a shopping mall, Klein could reach the masses and stay competitive with stores like The Gap and Banana Republic.

A "BRIDGE" COLLECTION

As Klein familiarized himself with malls and the tastes of people who shopped in them, he realized that his company was missing a middle-range line of women's clothes that appealed to this new generation of shoppers. His women's sportswear line, though reasonably priced, was not selling particularly well. Likewise, his top line of womenswear (which, incidentally, he and Schwartz still owned; they never licensed their top women's collection); the clothes were not selling well with middle-class women. Meanwhile, other designers were expanding into this middle-range line, called

Marci Klein attends an event with her father in 1998. It was Marci who suggested her father make clothes at a lower price point so her friends could afford them.

a "bridge" line, and experiencing great success. Donna Karan's DKNY collection, for example, was taking off. Other designers like Anne Klein and Ellen Tracy were doing similar things. In 1992, Klein was quoted as saying, "the future is in bridge."

Klein noticed another trend as well. The popularity of shopping malls and the enthusiastic response to Marky Mark and Kate Moss told him that his new collection had to be *young*. Indeed, his own daughter Marci, then in her twenties, was telling her father that most of her friends couldn't afford his clothes. Where was the line of clothes for people in her generation? She had a point, Klein thought. So not only did Klein need an affordable, middle-range collection for women *and* men, but he had to reach the young buyers' market. Klein had to develop a compelling new bridge collection that would satisfy them all.

cK

Klein's new cK collection, which debuted in 1993, marked a major change in direction in a number of ways. The clothes themselves were simpler and less expensive-looking than their counterparts in his top-line men's and women's collections, though they retained the Klein colors of black and gray. There was even a cK peacoat. Second, the models used in the advertisements didn't look like typical models. They looked like people one would see during a regular day—the guy sitting next to you in class, the girl on the bus or subway. Also, the images in the ads were more inclusive as men and women of color were finally represented in Klein's ad campaigns. Klein took this new direction so seriously that rumors circulated that he had real people mixed in with the professional models for the cK runway show.

Real was the word on everyone's lips, and the cK line was designed expressly for "real" people. In its review of the collection, the *New York Times* remarked that "every one of the models could have walked off the runway and into the street without anyone batting an eye." Everyone agrees today that the launch of cK was

ELEMENTS OF STYLE

"[The cK collection has] the essence of what Calvin Klein is all about: it has the style, it has the spirit, and it even can be younger because the clothes are not so expensive, so we can have more fun with them." "[The man who wears cK] is a younger, cooler, hipper guy, the young executive, the young corporate guy who doesn't have a lot of money to spend on clothes—and the clothes are more casual, [there's] lots of sportswear in the cK collection. [cK] clothes were meant for my daughter and her generation, but what I've discovered is all women are wearing them, because everyone . . . likes things that are casual and not so serious, so I'm appealing to a wide range of men and women with cK."

Calvin Klein in The Designers

a milestone in Klein's career, but many knew it at the time, too. In 1993, Klein was named Womenswear Designer of the Year and Menswear Designer of the Year by the Council of Fashion Designers of America. Klein himself knew it as well: "I felt this collection was a turning point. It's so right for people of all ages," he said.

cK one

Interestingly, the signature piece in the cK collection was not a piece of clothing, it was a fragrance. Introduced in 1994 and named "cK one" by none other than Klein himself, the scent was fruity, spicy, and light. Gone was the heaviness of Eternity and Escape, either of which could last for hours on one's skin. cK one smelled fresh and clean. Perhaps most significantly, cK one was intended for both men and women, which boosted sales. Its packaging was simple, too. In short, cK one was a total departure from previous Calvin Klein fragrances. In fact, it was different from most other fragrances on the market.

Klein was targeting young people for the entire cK line, including cK one. Just as was done for Obsession, Eternity, and Escape, a massive ad campaign was launched for cK one. Kate Moss was kept on as one of the models for the campaign, and they added other young actors and actresses as well. Klein's team also came up with a radical new idea to sell the scent at music stores and other places where young people hung out. The idea was a brilliant one, and stores that carried cK one completely sold out of their stock almost immediately. Klein had done it again. He reinvented a long-established part of the industry and hit a huge home run.

KLEIN'S MOST SERIOUS CONTROVERSY

As Klein celebrated the success of cK one, his team was preparing the advertising campaign for a new line of cK jeans and underwear geared toward teenagers. By now, everyone agreed that if Klein was not the most innovative fashion designer who ever lived, he was an utter genius at knowing his customer, what his customer would buy, and, most importantly, what his customer would buy *next*. He had proved this time and time again throughout his career. Furthermore, Klein, who turned 50 in 1992, had not lost his knack for knowing what younger generations were feeling and buying. Nowhere was this special sense more on display than his ads for cK jeans and underwear.

Both the television and print ads featured a mixture of real teenagers and teen actors being interviewed in the basement of a house. The commercials had a very 1970s feel, complete with wood-paneled walls and shag carpeting. In the ads, the teens were posing and behaving in very provocative ways. In one, a boy is asked by the off-camera interviewer to show how strong he is, and he promptly rips his cK T-shirt into pieces and tosses it on the floor, revealing his bare chest. Added to this was a raw, "home movie" feel that made the ads seem like auditions for pornographic films—but starring teenagers.

The successful ad campaign for cK one cologne featured teenagers and offered e-mail addresses for the characters they played. Although some considered Klein a genius for pushing the envelope, others questioned whether he was romanticizing child pornography.

Reaction to the ads was swift and unanimous. Predictably, parents and morality-oriented groups screamed in outrage. *Seventeen* magazine refused to run the print ads. A few politicians organized a boycott of the clothes. At first, Klein stuck to his guns and defended the ads. "We are stunned that anyone could find these ads pornographic," a statement from the company read. "If someone finds that these ads are pornographic, then they are reading something into them that was never intended ... the whole point of [the ads] is that people, regular people from anywhere ... have glamour inside of them." Eventually, however, the bad publicity started to make Klein nervous—he didn't want his brand tarnished—and the ads were taken off the air.

But that was not enough for some. Various organizations demanded to know if the models were actually under the age of 18. The controversy became even more serious when the federal government got involved. The U.S. Department of Justice began an official investigation into the ads. Even President Bill Clinton made his opinion known: "Those children [in the ads] were my daughter's age ... they were outrageous. It was wrong to manipulate those children and use them for commercial benefit." While the investigation ultimately did not find any illegal activity, the damage to Klein's reputation was done.

Klein reflected on the controversy some years later: "People didn't get that it's about modern young people who have an independent spirit and do the things they want to and can't be told or sold. None of that came through." Klein's wrists had been slapped, yet his ads would only get more provocative and explicit as the years went on. The apparent age of his models, however, was never again as ambiguous as in the cK campaign.

cK be

If anyone thought that Klein would follow this difficult period with something more innocent, they didn't know Calvin Klein very well. The advertising campaign for his next fragrance, called cK be, was more elaborate and just as controversial. This time it was not the age of the models that was questioned, but their physical appearance. The models used for the cK be ads were extremely thin—alarmingly so, in fact. Some critics thought they looked sick or perhaps under the influence of drugs. The models were tattooed and pierced as well, which contributed to the idea that these young people were dangerous or troubled. Again, groups objected to the ads. Though the ads may have reflected the reality that young people experimented with drugs, people said, it was wrong to use such images to sell a product. There was a general opinion that the ads encouraged kids to experiment with drugs. President Clinton commented on these ads, too: "The glorification of narcotics is not creative; it's destructive." Yet the controversy did not hurt sales. In fact, sales for all cK products remained extremely brisk even in the face of all the controversies.

9

Exiting the Stage

In the late 1990s, Klein continued to expand all his collections as he found himself, along with Ralph Lauren
and Donna Karan, leading the highly profitable American ready-to-wear market. Based in New York, these three designers defined a certain 1990s style that was sophisticated and casual,
practical and chic. The clothes' influences were varied: Klein's 1995
collection was inspired by 1950s actress Grace Kelly; the 1996
men's line was all black; by 1998, he was creating looks inspired
by the Japanese art of origami. Yet whatever fun he was having
designing new collections, there were new troubles on the horizon.
By this time, Klein had licensed almost every part of his design
empire, and he was beginning to have difficulty controlling his
brand.

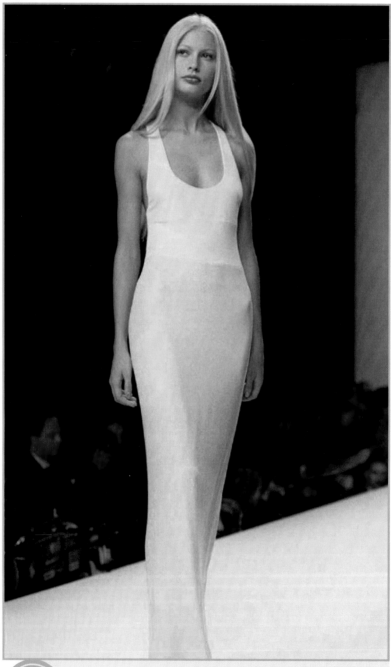

In the later years of his designing career, Klein expanded his ideas, but his original style remained. This dress from his 1996 collection epitomized Klein's understated chic.

NEW LICENSES

Klein and Schwartz sold the men's and women's underwear divisions in 1994 to a company named Warnaco. Warnaco was run by a tough, all-business woman named Linda Wachner. Warnaco owned licenses with companies as diverse as Ralph Lauren and Valentino. Warnaco had a strong reputation in the industry. In the deal that was struck, Warnaco would completely own the men's underwear division, as well as the licenses for men's accessories and women's underwear. Klein and Schwartz earned $64 million in royalties and up-front fees as part of the deal, and, more importantly, they were finally completely out of debt.

The deal with Warnaco signaled a shift for Klein and Schwartz that had been brewing for a number of years. Calvin Klein, Inc., was not going to do any more of its own manufacturing or sales. Just about every collection under the Calvin Klein label was going to be licensed. Almost immediately after the Warnaco deal for underwear, Klein and Schwartz sold the license for Calvin Klein jeans to a company called Rio Sportswear. The men made $50 million on that deal. Also created was a line of home products called Calvin Klein Home that included furniture, linens, and wallpaper. It was licensed to a company called Home Innovations, Inc.

TOO MUCH POWER?

After Warnaco had a number of years of excellent sales, Linda Wachner got the idea to buy Rio Sportswear. Rio Sportswear had hit some hard times by 1997 and was ripe for a takeover. After the purchase, suddenly Wachner was in control of Calvin Klein jeans and underwear, two of Klein's most profitable and signature lines. Ownership equals power, and the result of one licensee (in this case, Warnaco) owning so many of a company's licenses is that the licensee may end up having more influence on the direction of the company than the owners of the company themselves. Klein and Schwartz were beginning to worry that Linda Wachner was going to take Calvin Klein, Inc., in directions they didn't like.

ANOTHER CONTROVERSY

As their concern mounted, the launch of yet another line was met with controversy, this time Calvin Klein Underwear for Kids. The seemingly wholesome ads of children running around a house wearing nothing but their underwear, were, in light of the cK controversy, seen as inappropriate. Nothing could be further from the truth, but Klein now had a questionable reputation and was thus an easy target for criticism. When television personality Rosie O'Donnell voiced her objection to the ads on her hit daytime talk show, a stunning decision was made: The entire campaign would be canceled. About this controversy, again Klein defended himself: "I don't set out, and we as a company don't set out, to have something become controversial . . . the goal is to be inventive, creative, on the edge, always thinking about young people and what they might think is cool and of the moment and sometimes provocative. . . . So that could add up to controversy."

GLOBAL EXPANSION

A major change in the structure of the company occurred in 1994 when Klein and Schwartz hired a woman named Gabriella Forte to be the new president and chief operating officer. The hiring of Forte signaled that Klein was ready to expand the global reach of his brand. Almost immediately after Forte came on board, Calvin Klein Japan and Calvin Klein Europe were created with licenses for all of Klein's clothes, fragrances, and accessories. There were Calvin Klein stores in London, Paris, Rome, Milan, and Korea. It was an enormous expansion, and it happened very fast. Some people at the company worried that it might be too much to manage, but Forte, Klein, and Schwartz stuck to their global vision for the Calvin Klein brand. They were determined to make it work.

FLAGSHIP STORE

Amazingly, for all its worldwide reach and in-store boutiques, Calvin Klein, Inc., did not have a main store, called a flagship store, in

New York City. That finally changed in 1995 amid all the success of the cK line. The time seemed right. Located on Madison Avenue, the 20,000-square-foot (1,858-square-meter) Calvin Klein store consists of four levels of clothes, jeans, underwear, accessories, and home furnishings. However, it only features products from Klein's most expensive, high-end line, the Calvin Klein Collection. Klein also uses the store for fashion shows to introduce new collections.

Not surprisingly, the store itself has a minimalist design—so much so that the *New York Times* once described it as having a "spare parking-garage design." Indeed, visitors are immediately struck by the clean, simple design elements that showcase Klein's classic, neutral-colored clothes. The store even features minimalist

In 1995, Calvin Klein opened a flagship store on New York City's Madison Avenue. The architecture of the store complements the clean, minimal style of Klein's fashion and home design products.

furniture designed by American artist Donald Judd. On the top floor, one can look out on a magnificent view of New York's busy Madison Avenue, home to all the greatest designers in the world.

CALVIN KLEIN FOR SALE

With Calvin Klein, Inc., leading the way, the late 1990s were an extremely prosperous period for fashion design companies. By this time, large corporations had bought their way into the industry in an attempt to make money and broaden the global reach of their brands. For example, the liquor company Moët Hennessy, maker of fine champagnes and cognacs, purchased handbag designer Louis Vuitton in 1987. A number of design companies either merged with other companies during this period or were acquired outright. For Calvin Klein, Inc., its greatest year was 1997, when it took in more than $5 billion in worldwide sales—an astonishing amount.

Klein and Schwartz took advantage of this corporate craze and put Calvin Klein, Inc., up for sale in 1999. Not surprisingly, there were many interested parties. Design companies like Gucci, Prada, Tommy Hilfiger, and others were in the running to buy the company. The idea of purchasing Calvin Klein, Inc., was particularly appealing to Warnaco's Linda Wachner, for if she owned Calvin Klein, Inc., she would own the name, meaning she would no longer have to pay Klein and Schwartz's big royalty fees. Wachner made an offer that Klein and Schwartz felt was too small, and Warnaco walked away from a possible deal. After a period of other offers, Klein and Schwartz felt the opportunity to sell the company had passed, and they withdrew the company from consideration.

A HIGH-PROFILE DISPUTE

Though Linda Wachner had passed on buying the company, she was still the most important player in Klein's empire other than Barry Schwartz. Her company, Warnaco, was still the major license holder, and her jeans and underwear divisions accounted for some $60 million in annual sales. Klein and Schwartz were not entirely happy with

Worn by the Rich and Famous

Designers gain attention and win new admirers when a celebrity wears their clothes. Calvin Klein has been particularly fortunate in this way, with many famous women modeling his designs over the years. While Brooke Shields, Marky Mark, and Kate Moss were paid to wear his clothes, his visibility increased on other occasions thanks to celebrities. For example, when actress Amy Ryan was an Oscar nominee for best supporting actress in 2008, she wore a gorgeous dark blue gown by Klein to the ceremony. Hundreds of photographs were taken of Ryan in her Calvin Klein dress. Other celebrities who are known for wearing Calvin Klein are Kerry Washington, Kate Bosworth, Eva Mendes, Gwyneth Paltrow, and no fewer than three first ladies: Jacqueline Kennedy Onassis, Nancy Reagan, and Michelle Obama. One famous woman who came to be strongly associated with Klein was Carolyn Bessette. Before she became famous for marrying John F. Kennedy Jr., Bessette worked for Klein, first as a saleswoman and then in the company's public relations department. Bessette, who was blond, slim, and attractive, wore clothes from both Klein's women's collection and his new cK line to the office. Her daily wardrobe made such an impression that soon every woman in the PR department was dressing like her. After she married Kennedy, the most eligible bachelor in the country, her visibility intensified. The couple was constantly photographed at social events, gallery openings, and theater premieres, and Bessette was almost always wearing Calvin Klein.

Wachner. She had begun to do things that Klein felt were hurting the image of Calvin Klein clothes. For example, she allowed Calvin Klein underwear to be sold at J.C. Penney, a department store that did not have the same high profile as Macy's or Bloomingdale's.

Did Wachner have the legal right to offer Calvin Klein underwear and jeans to stores like J.C. Penney? It was an important question that soon became a fierce argument, and in 2000, Klein and Schwartz sued Wachner in an effort to end their business relationship. The two men claimed they had asked her many times to stop allowing low-end stores to sell Calvin Klein products. It would come out in the lawsuit that she had even sold some Calvin Klein products to warehouse stores like Costco and Sam's Club. Her contract apparently allowed for discontinued clothes to be sold to those kinds of stores, but not new products, which were reserved for Macy's, Bloomingdale's, and similar high-end stores. Other complaints had to do with Wachner changing Klein's designs without his permission and selling other designers' jeans and underwear in Calvin Klein outlet stores. Klein appeared on the television program *Larry King Live* in 2000 and asserted, "It's important that when the consumer [buys] any of the jeans wear product that they know that it is our design. . . . Much of the product that's out there did not meet our specifications and product was altered and designed." The lawsuit had a decidedly unkind and personal tone, with the two men even calling her "a cancer on the value and integrity" of the Calvin Klein brand.

Wachner attacked Klein in her own defense. She said that Klein had not really designed the jeans that her company controlled and, further, that he hadn't designed much of anything for many years. She painted a portrait of Klein as totally disengaged with the running of his design empire. "Since 1999," she claimed in her defense, "Mr. Klein has had no visible or apparent personal involvement in the design of Calvin Klein jeanswear or underwear." She also touched a sore spot when she referenced the controversies surrounding the cK ads. She argued that the ads were hurting sales of all Calvin Klein products, of which jeans and underwear were her responsibility.

BAD PUBLICITY

There was an unintended and unwanted side effect of the lawsuit. The trial exposed details about Calvin Klein, Inc., that were unflattering. People in the fashion industry learned from the lawsuit that Klein's business had been experiencing difficulties in recent years—something that many had suspected but could never confirm. Now the facts were out on the table. If Klein was saying that Wachner was responsible for the design of his jeans, then what else did he not have control of? It was a lot of unwanted bad publicity.

When the trial began on January 22, 2001, it quickly became the most high-profile, high-stakes lawsuit in the history of the fashion business. Everyone was gearing up for what was sure to be a long, dramatic fight for the future of America's most famous designer. But it was not to be. Klein and Wachner came to a settlement, which meant that there would be no trial. The details of the agreement were confidential, but some people who were in a position to know about them told the press that Wachner could keep the license for Calvin Klein jeans as long as she agreed to reduce the number of discount stores she sold to. Klein, as ever, reaffirmed his control of the design of all products, including those for which she owned the licenses. In an unfortunate final chapter to the drama, Warnaco would file for bankruptcy just five months later, and Linda Wachner would be removed as head of the company.

LOSS OF LUSTER

People were divided in their opinions about whether the Calvin Klein brand had suffered as a result of all the bad publicity surrounding the Warnaco lawsuit. What could not be argued, however, is that business was suffering. For example, Calvin Klein Japan had closed its doors at the end of 1999, and other foreign divisions of the company were not performing well. In 2001, the main cK bridge line, the sportswear line, was discontinued. Klein and Schwartz wanted to get back to what got them started in the early years: high-end collections for men and women. The emphasis on youth was being reduced.

With the decision to eliminate the main bridge line, Calvin Klein found itself in a challenging position in the fashion marketplace. On the one hand, the Calvin Klein name, while somewhat damaged, was still a powerful draw for high-end customers. On the other hand, designers like Liz Claiborne and Phillips-Van Heusen were dominating the bridge market that Klein had recently abandoned. And to complicate things even further, it was becoming easier and easier for consumers to buy cheap versions of high-end fashions. Stores like Target were hiring name designers to introduce inexpensive collections for sale exclusively at their discount stores. Also, European stores like H&M and Zara were offering their own cheap versions of high-end fashions. People didn't have to pay a lot at Calvin Klein to look fashionable—they could just go to Target or H&M.

PHILLIPS–VAN HEUSEN

One of the effects of the Warnaco bankruptcy was that many of its licenses were available for purchase, which meant that Klein and Schwartz suddenly had a chance to buy back their jeans and underwear lines. But they weren't the only people interested.

Phillips-Van Heusen was a company well known for its specialization in men's shirts. Its history went back to the late nineteenth century, when Moses Phillips sold his hand-sewn shirts to local miners in Pittsburgh, Pennsylvania. The company eventually became the manufacturer of many of the most famous shirt brands in the world: Izod, Arrow, Geoffrey Beene, Kenneth Cole, and its own Van Heusen line. It was a company that was in the business of acquiring famous brands of men's shirts, and Calvin Klein was on its target list.

In 2002, Phillips Van-Heusen, or PVH, won the license to manufacture Calvin Klein men's dress shirts. It was an extremely successful partnership, one bright spot in the middle of an overall shrinking of the Calvin Klein company. Bruce Klatsky, the head of PVH, naturally wanted more—indeed, he wanted to buy all of Calvin Klein, Inc. Klein and Schwartz began talking to Klatsky and the PVH people about a potential sale later that year. Despite sales of about $3 billion a year, Calvin Klein, Inc., was losing a lot of money by the early 2000s. It says a lot about the strength of the Calvin Klein brand that PVH would want to purchase a company that was losing somewhere between $30 million and $50 million a year.

A monumental day had finally arrived. A deal to sell Calvin Klein, Inc., to Phillips-Van Heusen was announced on December 17, 2002. PVH would own the Calvin Klein brand, business, and licenses. Klein and Schwartz were going to make a fortune: The sale price was $400 million in cash and $30 million in PVH stock. There was also a deal for future royalties that would be earned on the Calvin Klein brand name that would bring Klein and Schwartz an additional $300 million. Klatsky said that his first task as the new head of Calvin Klein was to launch men's and women's sportswear lines. He also wanted to take another look at the foreign markets that Klein had abandoned earlier in the decade.

MOVING ON

After the sale to PVH, Barry Schwartz retired. He wanted to spend more time with his other great passion, horse racing. Schwartz is chairman of the board for the New York Racing Association, an organization that operates three large horse-racing tracks in New York State.

For Calvin Klein, the one thing that he had always insisted on having was creative control over the designs that bore his name. So it was seen as a significant detail when such control was not specifically included in the deal with PVH. Many in the fashion world saw it as an end of an era. The final collection that Klein personally oversaw debuted on February 14, 2003. Klein did promise to oversee other aspects of the company until 2006, but today he is, in his words, "completely free."

PERSONAL LIFE

Since leaving the day-to-day operation of Calvin Klein, Inc., Klein's personal life has been, by all accounts, pleasurable and satisfying, despite divorcing Kelly in 2006, after a decade of living apart. For the first time in his life, he has time to pursue other passions and interests. He spent four years designing a new apartment in New York that is—no surprise—minimalist in its design. He also is interested in architecture and may someday write a book about his life. He spends time designing furniture and collecting art, photographs, and rare books.

NEW CREATIVE DIRECTORS

In 2002, as he was preparing his company for sale, Klein hired new creative directors. These new designers have slowly introduced some changes to the traditional Calvin Klein look. The long-established color palette has been expanded to include some surprises.

Today, the man in charge of the entire company is named Kevin Carrigan. In addition to managing all the licenses, Carrigan oversees the sportswear and cK collections.

FRANCISCO COSTA

Francisco Costa is the head designer for the womenswear collection. Costa was born in a small town in Brazil and, like Klein,

After Klein's retirement, Francisco Costa (*above*) was named head designer of Calvin Klein womenswear. While adhering to the Calvin Klein aesthetic, Costa has expanded the label's look.

graduated from FIT. After working for Bill Blass and Oscar de la Renta, Costa went to work at Gucci, where he acquired a reputation for being able to handle the most important collections of a major designer. He continues to use those skills today at Calvin Klein, Inc. His designs are in keeping with the classic Calvin Klein look. Costa describes his work as "eclectic, but consistent," as he "absorbs influences from all areas of our world and our environment." Costa has been highly praised; his 2004 collection was called "the single best collection of the spring shows" by the *New York Times*, and he won CFDA Womenswear Designer of the year in 2006 and 2008, following in the footsteps of Calvin Klein himself.

ITALO ZUCCHELLI

In 2003, Klein named a new design director for the menswear line. Italo Zucchelli, an Italian, worked for Klein for four years before being named to his current position. As a young man in Italy, Zucchelli remembers seeing Klein's men's underwear advertisements featuring Tom Hintnaus. Zucchelli, author David Lamb writes, has an "inherent sense of sophisticated cool that has not only met with critical acclaim, but is an honest continuation of the Calvin Klein brand philosophy." Zucchelli has also been gaining attention for his bold moves away from Klein's traditional neutral colors. His spring 2009 runway show featured a men's suit in the color of a cherry popsicle! His designs have reenergized the men's collection at Calvin Klein.

Though Klein himself had a reduced role, Calvin Klein, Inc., was still breaking new ground and, as always, licensing was part of it. In 2004, a license was signed for a new line of outerwear, and in 2005, a new licensing agreement was made with a company named Fingen S.p.A. to manufacture and sell the top men's and women's lines. Other licenses ensured an even larger global reach for the Calvin Klein brand, which shows no sign of slowing down. The newest products to bear the Calvin Klein name include a line of furniture that was launched in 2008; in 2009, a new men's

My design philosophy is as simple as it is unchanging. I believe in purity, minimalism, and above all, clothes that are modern. Real. Fluid. Clean. Free. Devoid of affection. These ideas stem from a growing perception of global change. This movement has to do with the changing reality of who we are. And, we are no longer about excess. Our changing mindset is personified by a new kind of beauty. It's less perfect, more real, more sense.

Calvin Klein in Paolo Luchetta + RetailDesign: Works 1999–2006

[Beauty is] my life's quest. I need to be surrounded by beauty on a daily basis, and it's what drives my work. I've always tried to make people beautiful and attractive with my clothes and to showcase the bodies that excited me in my ad campaigns. Men, women, fashion, furniture—beauty is what moves me the most.

Calvin Klein in Vogue Homme International

fragrance, ck free, was released. October 2010 saw the debut of a new women's scent called Beauty.

In a 2007 interview, Klein talked about handing over his design responsibilities to new people: "There's always a risk that the people who come after you don't understand, or don't subscribe to what you've accomplished. The upside is that they can take the company places that you never explored yourself. In this kind of handover, some of it is gratifying and, inevitably, some of it is disappointing. You have to know when to let go."

A PLACE IN FASHION HISTORY

Though Calvin Klein's place in fashion history is secure, there is debate as to whether he will be remembered as a great designer or as the head of a global design empire. As a designer, there is no mistaking his distinctive minimalist style that has endured for more than 40 years. Yet Klein is not known for a specific "look" or for a particular dress, though his dresses are in the fashion collections of many great museums.

The chief fashion writer for the *New York Times*, Caryn Horyn, discussed Klein's legacy in an extensive profile she wrote in 2003: "Klein ... did not create an indelible fashion mark, in the way that Giorgio Armani and [Yves] Saint Laurent did. ... But in a way, it wasn't about the clothes. You may not remember the cut of a Calvin Klein jacket, but you will remember Brooke Shields rolling up on her back to talk about her 'Calvins,' or Kate Moss ... in the Obsession ads, or Marky Mark. ... In the simplest terms, Klein's genius was to shift the conversation from being one purely about fashion (what I wear) to attitude (how I look). And in doing that, he changed the whole game." So while some writers like Horyn feel Klein's desire to appeal to the masses tended to weaken his designer's eye, others argue the opposite: It's not easy to create a classic, American look that stretches across every genre of fashion.

It is an interesting argument that has no easy answer and promises to go on for as long as people study the great fashion designers of the twentieth century. Perhaps it can be said that Calvin Klein is actually *both*: the greatest fashion designer America has ever produced *and* a man who built the most far-reaching and well-known fashion empire the world has ever seen.

Chronology

1942	Calvin Klein born on November 18 in the Bronx, New York.
1963	Earns fine arts degree from the Fashion Institute of Technology (FIT).
1964	Marries Jayne Centre.
1967	Daughter, Marci, is born.
1968	Forms Calvin Klein, Ltd., with partner Barry Schwartz.

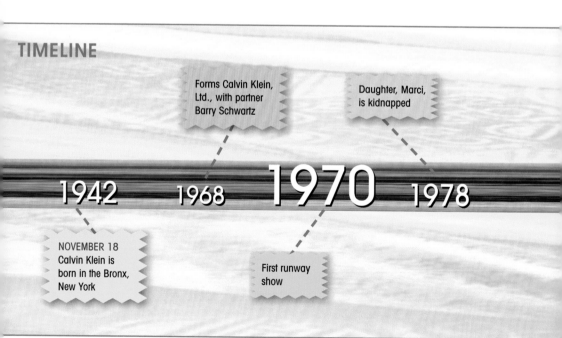

TIMELINE

Forms Calvin Klein, Ltd., with partner Barry Schwartz

Daughter, Marci, is kidnapped

1942   1968   **1970**   1978

NOVEMBER 18
Calvin Klein is born in the Bronx, New York

First runway show

1970	First runway show.
1973	Wins first of three consecutive Coty American Fashion Critics Awards ("Winnie").
1978	Daughter, Marci, is kidnapped.
1980	Calvin Klein jeans ads featuring Brooke Shields first appear in August.
1985	Debut of Obsession fragrance.
1986	Marries Kelly Rector.
1993	Wins Menswear Designer of the Year and Womenswear Designer of the Year from the Council of Fashion Designers of America (CFDA).
	Launch of cK collection.
1995	Opens flagship Calvin Klein Collection store on Madison Avenue in New York City.

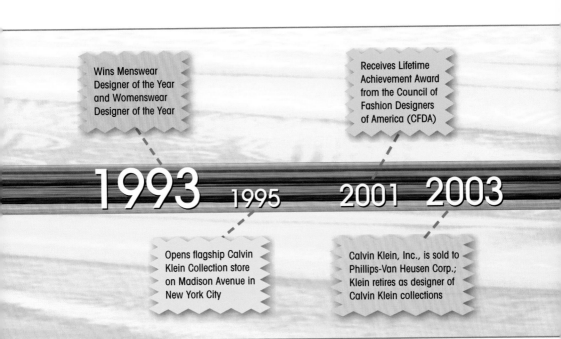

Wins Menswear Designer of the Year and Womenswear Designer of the Year

Receives Lifetime Achievement Award from the Council of Fashion Designers of America (CFDA)

1993   1995   2001   **2003**

Opens flagship Calvin Klein Collection store on Madison Avenue in New York City

Calvin Klein, Inc., is sold to Phillips-Van Heusen Corp.; Klein retires as designer of Calvin Klein collections

2001	Receives Lifetime Achievement Award from the Council of Fashion Designers of America (CFDA).
2003	Calvin Klein, Inc., is sold to Phillips-Van Heusen Corp.; Klein retires as designer of Calvin Klein collections.
2008	Launch of Calvin Klein Furniture collection.

Glossary

aloof   Distant, detached, or snobbish.

bankruptcy   When a person or company runs out of money and can't pay its debts.

bar mitzvah   A ceremony in which a 13-year-old boy is admitted to the Jewish community as an adult.

borough   An incorporated division of a city.

boycott   An organized protest that occurs when people get together and agree not to patronize a business.

branding   The way a company uses its name, logo, and product design to promote and publicize itself.

caftan   A long, robelike garment of Middle Eastern origin that is tied at the waist and has wide sleeves.

couture   High-quality, high-fashion, custom-made clothing.

couturier   Someone who designs fashions for women.

eclectic   Influenced by a variety of sources.

elope   To run off and get married in secret.

emigrant   Someone who leaves his or her home country to live in another country.

gaudy   Flashy, showy, and usually in poor taste.

gregarious   Social, friendly, and extroverted.

iconic   When something is so distinctive and important that it becomes a symbol of a larger idea or concept.

integral Absolutely essential to something bigger.

licensee A person or company that buys the right to use another person or company's name or image.

licensing The practice of allowing another company to use one's name, design, or logo in exchange for a fee, called a royalty.

licensor A person or company that allows another person or company to use its name or image in exchange for a fee.

lucrative Profitable and moneymaking.

marketing All of a company's activities related to the buying and selling of a product.

mentor Someone who counsels or teaches someone else, usually an older, wiser person.

minimalism A design style that is characterized by refinement, restraint, and elegance.

mural A large picture painted directly on a wall.

novel New and different.

perfectionistic Trying to do everything exactly right or perfectly.

protégé A person who is under the supervision of someone who is supportive of his or her work and career.

ransom Holding a person against his or her will in exchange for money.

ready-to-wear Clothing that is mass-produced in standard sizes and can be bought off a store rack.

rift A break in friendship between people.

royalty The fee a licensee pays to a licensor for the right to use a name or image.

seamstress A woman who sews for a living.

silhouette In fashion design, the outline or shape of a dress.

synagogue A Jewish place of worship.

synthetic   Human-made, artificial.

tunic   A plain jacket typically worn with a belt around the waist that has had many styles over the years; it can be sleeved or sleeveless, short or long skirted, and worn by men or women.

unpretentious   Modest, humble, and plain.

Bibliography

"1985—Calvin Klein's Obsession." Video clip. 1985. http://www. youtube.com/watch?v=PjH9YsKZTp0 (accessed June 20, 2010).

Adams, Bryan. *American Women.* Brooklyn, N.Y.: powerHouse Books, 2005.

Agins, Teri. *The End of Fashion.* New York: William Morrow and Company, Inc., 1999.

The Art Students League of New York. "About Us." http://www. theartstudentsleague.org/about.html (accessed April 30, 2010).

Baudot, François. *Fashion: The Twentieth Century.* Rev. ed. New York: Universe Publishing, 2006.

Baxter-Wright, Emma. *Vintage Fashion: Collecting and Wearing Vintage Classics, 1900–1990.* New York: Collins Design, 2007.

Blackman, Cally. *One Hundred Years of Menswear.* London: Laurence King Publishing, 2009.

Bois, Yve-Alain. "Specific Objections." *Artforum.* Summer 2004. http://artforum.com/inprint/id=6955 (accessed July 8, 2010).

Breward, Christopher. *The Culture of Fashion.* New York: Manchester University Press, 1995.

Bryan, Robert E. *American Fashion Menswear.* New York: Assouline Publishing, 2009.

Buxbaum, Gerda, ed. *Icons of Fashion: The 20th Century.* New York: Prestel, 2005.

Calvin Klein, Inc. http://www.calvinkleininc.com/ (accessed April 1, 2010).

"Calvin Klein 'Obsession' Commercial (1985)." Video clip. 1985. http://www.youtube.com/watch?v=h7UHA_tr7S0&feature= related (accessed June 20, 2010).

"Calvin Klein 'Obsession' Commercial with Lazarus Tag." Video clip. c. 1989. http://www.youtube.com/watch?v=mYAFI-EJBQA (accessed June 20, 2010).

Craven, Jo. "Calvin Klein." *Vogue,* April 22, 2008. http://www.vogue.co.uk/biographies/080422-calvin-klein-biography.aspx (accessed May 1, 2010).

Davies, Dean Mayo. "Calvin Klein and the Underwear Revolution." *Ponystep,* December 31, 2008. http://www.ponystep.com/article/CalvinKleinandtheunderwearrevolution_239.aspx (accessed June 15, 2010).

The Designers. Vol. 13, Calvin Klein. DVD. New York: Videofashion Network, Inc., 1999.

"Diane Kruger for Calvin Klein 'Beauty' Fragrance." Fashion Copious: A Fashion Blog. May 7, 2010. http://fashioncopious.typepad.com/fashioncopious/2010/05/diane-kruger-for-calvin-klein-beauty-fragrance.html (accessed July 12, 2010).

DiMaria, Eugene. "Moet-Vuitton: A Luxe Combo." *Womenswear Daily,* July 10, 1987. http://www.accessmylibrary.com/article-1G1-5036927/moet-vuitton-luxe-combo.html (accessed June 10, 2010).

Downey, Lynn. *A Short History of Denim.* Levi Strauss & Co., 2007. http://www.levistrauss.com/sites/default/files/library document/2010/4/History-Denim.pdf (accessed May 30, 2010).

Encyclopaedia Britannica Online, s.v. "Calvin Klein." http://search.eb.com/eb/article-9045732 (accessed June 1, 2010).

English, Bonnie. *A Cultural History of Fashion in the 20th Century.* New York: Berg, 2007.

———. *Fashion: The 50 Most Influential Fashion Designers of All Time.* London: Elwin Street Limited, 2009.

Erlanger, Steven. "France Salutes the Ultimate Couturier." *New York Times,* June 6, 2008. http://www.nytimes.com/2008/06/06/world/europe/06ysl.html?_r=2&hp&oref=slogin (accessed June 10, 2010).

Ernest Klein & Company International Supermarket. http://www. ernestklein.net/kleinhome.php (accessed April 30, 2010).

Ewing, Elizabeth. *History of 20th Century Fashion.* Revised by Alice Mackrell. Hollywood, Calif.: Costume & Fashion Press, 2001.

Fashion Institute of Technology. "The History." http://www.fitnyc. edu/1807.asp (accessed May 15, 2010).

————. "Undergraduate Programs." http://www.fitnyc.edu/1706. asp (accessed May 15, 2010).

Five Dances by Martha Graham. "Maple Leaf Rag." VHS. Produced by Martha Graham Dance Company, Cameras Continentales, LA SEPT in association with BBC, Fiona Morris, producer. Directed by Peter Mumford. Netherlands: Philips, c. 1994.

Gaines, Steven, and Sharon Churcher. *Obsession: The Lives and Times of Calvin Klein.* New York: Birch Lane Press, 1994.

Golbin, Pamela. *Fashion Designers.* New York: Watson-Guptill Publications, 2001.

Heimann, Jim, and Alison A. Nieder. *20th Century Fashion: 100 Years of Apparel Ads.* Cologne, Germany: Taschen, 2009.

The High School of Art and Design. http://www.artanddesignhs. com/ (accessed April 30, 2010).

Horyn, Cathy. "His Era Ending, Saint Laurent Decides to Take His Final Bow." *New York Times*, January 8, 2002. http://www. nytimes.com/2002/01/08/fashion/08YVES.html (accessed June 10, 2010).

————. "The Calvinist Ethic." *New York Times*, September 14, 2003. http://www.nytimes.com/2003/09/14/magazine/style-the-calvinist-ethic.html?ref=calvin_klein (accessed June 1, 2010).

————. "All the Pretty Clothes. And Then, Calvin Klein." *New York Times*, September 16, 2004. http://www.nytimes. com/2004/09/16/fashion/16DRES.html?ref=calvin_klein (accessed May 30, 2010).

Hulse, Bruce. *Sex, Love, and Fashion: A Memoir of a Male Model.* New York: Harmony Books, 2008.

*InStyle.*Fashion."Celeb-Inspired Dresses for Under $400: Amy Ryan in Calvin Klein." http://www.instyle.com/instyle/package/general/photos/0,,20182239_20181980_20420344,00.html (accessed June 10, 2010).

———. DesignerCentral: Calvin Klein. "Who's Wearing Calvin Klein." http://fashiondesigners.instyle.com/who_is_wearing/thumbs/calvin-klein/results.html (accessed June 10, 2010).

John Pawson, architect. Designer of Calvin Klein store in New York. http://www.johnpawson.com/architecture/stores/calvinklein/newyork/ (accessed July 8, 2010).

Jones, Terry, and Susie Rushton, eds. *Fashion Now 2.* Cologne, Germany: Taschen, 2005.

Junior High School 080 the Mosholu Parkway. http://schools.nyc.gov/SchoolPortals/10/X080/default.htm (accessed April 30, 2010).

Kennedy, Dana. "Fashion Show and Tell." *Entertainment Weekly,* May 20, 1994. http://www.ew.com/ew/article/0,,302273,00.html (accessed May 1, 2010).

Klein, Calvin. *collection.* New York: Calvin Klein, 1996.

———. *home.* New York: Calvin Klein, 1996.

———. Interview by Larry King. *Larry King Live.* CNN, June 5, 2000. http://quiz.cnn.com/TRANSCRIPTS/0006/05/lkl.00.html (accessed June 20, 2010).

———. Interview by Olivier Lalanne. *Vogue Hommes International* (Fall–Winter 2007–2008): 247–251.

———. Interview by Glenn Plaskin. In *The Playboy Interviews: Movers and Shakers,* edited by Stephen Randall and the editors of *Playboy,* 39–73. Milwaukie, Ore.: M Press, 2007.

Kyoto Costume Institute. *Fashion: A History from the 18th to the 20th Century.* Vol. 2. Cologne, Germany: Taschen, 2006.

Larocca, Amy. "The House of Mod." *New York,* Spring Fashion 2003. http://nymag.com/nymetro/shopping/fashion/spring03/n_8337/ (accessed June 1, 2010).

Laver, James. *Costume and Fashion: A Concise History.* New York: Thames & Hudson, 2002.

Lucchetta, Paolo + RetailDesign srl. *Works 1999–2006.* Milan, Italy: Mondadori Electa Spa, 2006.

MacKenzie, Mairi. *. . . Isms: Understanding Fashion.* London: Herbert Press, 2009.

Marsh, Lisa. *The House of Klein.* Hoboken, N.J.: John Wiley & Sons, Inc., 2003.

Martin, Richard. "Calvin Klein." Updated by Donna W. Reamy. Fashion Encyclopedia. http://www.fashionencyclopedia.com/Ki-Le/Klein-Calvin.html (accessed April 10, 2010).

Mulvagh, Jane. *Vogue History of 20th Century Fashion.* London: Penguin Group, 1988.

The New School University Libraries. Fashion Design History Database. "Claire McCardell." http://library.newschool.edu/speccoll/fashionhistory/mccardell.php (accessed May 15, 2010).

New York. Fashion. "Calvin Klein." http://nymag.com/fashion/fashionshows/designers/bios/calvinklein/ (accessed June 10, 2010).

The New York Racing Association. http://www.nyra.com/ (accessed June 20, 2010).

New York Times. "New Yorkers & Co." August 21, 1994. http://www.nytimes.com/1994/08/21/nyregion/new-yorkers-co-006807.html?ref=calvin_klein (accessed July 8, 2010).

———. *Times Topics: Calvin Klein.* http://topics.nytimes.com/topics/reference/timestopics/people/k/calvin_klein/index.html?scp=1-spot&sq=calvin%20klein&st=cse (accessed May 10, 2010).

———. *Times Topics: Yves Saint Laurent.* http://topics.nytimes.com/top/reference/timestopics/people/s/yves_saint_laurent/index.html?inline=nyt-per (accessed June 10, 2010).

O'Hara Callan, Georgina. *The Thames & Hudson Dictionary of Fashion and Fashion Designers.* Updated by Cat Glover. 2nd ed. New York: Thames & Hudson, 2008.

The Paradise Theater. "History of the Paradise." http://www.
paradisetheaterevents.com/index.php?option=com_content&
view=article&id=74&Itemid=78 (accessed April 30, 2010).

Phaidon Press. *The Fashion Book.* New York: Phaidon Press, 1998.

Phillips-Van Heusen Corporation. "The History of a Modern World-
Class Company." http://www.pvh.com/history.html (accessed
June 2, 2010).

Rozhon, Tracie. "Calvin Klein Selling His Company to Biggest
Shirtmaker in the U.S." *New York Times,* December 18, 2002.
http://www.nytimes.com/2002/12/18/business/calvin-klein-
selling-his-company-to-biggest-shirtmaker-in-the-us.html
(accessed June 1, 2010).

———. "Sure, It Lost Plenty of Money, but, Hey, It's Calvin Klein;
Owner Says the Golden Name Is the Bottom Line." *New York
Times,* October 3, 2003. http://www.nytimes.com/2003/10/03/
business/sure-it-lost-plenty-money-but-hey-it-s-calvin-
klein-owner-says-golden-name.html?ref=calvin_klein
(accessed July 7, 2010).

Saturday Night Live. "Canis." Transcript. *Saturday Night Live,*
Season 18: Episode 1. http://snltranscripts.jt.org/92/92acanis.
phtml (accessed June 25, 2010).

———. "Compulsion." Transcript. *Saturday Night Live,* Season
13: Episode 4. http://snltranscripts.jt.org/87/87dcompulsion.
phtml (accessed June 25, 2010).

Schiro, Anne-Marie. "Yves Saint Laurent, Fashion Icon, Dies at 71." *New
York Times,* June 1, 2008. http://www.nytimes.com/2008/06/01/
style/01cnd-laurent.html?_r=3 (accessed June 10, 2010).

Seaman, Margo. "Claire McCardell." Fashion Encyclopedia. http://
www.fashionencyclopedia.com/Ma-Mu/Mccardell-Claire.
html (accessed May 10, 2010).

Silver, Cameron. "The Travails of Shopping for a Fit Man's
Physique." *Huffington Post,* September 12, 2007. http://www.
huffingtonpost.com/cameron-silver/cameron-silver-the-
travai_b_64147.html (accessed July 8, 2010).

Spindler, Amy M. "Three Designers Struggle with Image." *New York Times,* November 4, 1995. http://www.nytimes.com/1995/11/04/style/review-fashion-three-designers-struggle-with-image.html?ref=calvin_klein (accessed July 5, 2010).

Steele, Valerie. *Fifty Years of Fashion.* New Haven, Conn.: Yale University Press, 1997.

————, ed. *Encyclopedia of Clothing and Fashion* (Scribner Library of Daily Life). 3 vols. Farmington, Minn.: Thomson Gale, 2005.

Sterlacci, Francesca, and Joanne Arbuckle. *Historical Dictionary of the Fashion Industry.* Lanham, Md.: Scarecrow Press, 2008.

Stilson, Sam. "The Perfection of the Pea Coat." The Soko. http://thesoko.com/thesoko/article1262.html (accessed April 20, 2010).

Style.com "Calvin Klein." http://www.style.com/fashionshows/designerdirectory/CKLEIN/seasons/ (accessed May 10, 2010).

Sullivan, James. *Jeans: A Cultural History of an American Icon.* New York: Gotham Books, 2006.

Suqi, Rima. "Calvin Klein's Clean Lines, Now in Wood." *New York Times,* October 15, 2008. http://www.nytimes.com/2008/10/16/garden/16goods.html?ref=calvin_klein (accessed June 15, 2010).

Wadler, Joyce. "Calvin Klein's Partner Defines a Long Shot." *New York Times,* April 21, 1999. http://www.nytimes.com/1999/04/21/nyregion/public-lives-calvin-klein-s-partner-defines-a-long-shot.html?sec=&spon=&pagewanted=all (accessed May 15, 2010).

Watson, Linda. *20th Century Fashion.* New York: Firefly Books, Ltd., 2004.

White, Constance C.R. "For CK, a Big Step in a New Direction." *New York Times,* February 28, 1995. http://www.nytimes.com/1995/02/28/style/review-fashion-for-ck-a-big-step-in-a-new-direction.html?ref=calvin_klein (accessed July 2, 2010).

Further Resources

BOOKS

Baudot, François. *Fashion: The Twentieth Century.* Rev. ed. New York: Universe Publishing, 2006.

Baxter-Wright, Emma. *Vintage Fashion: Collecting and Wearing Vintage Classics, 1900–1990.* New York: Collins Design, 2007.

English, Bonnie. *A Cultural History of Fashion in the 20th Century.* New York: Berg, 2007.

Ewing, Elizabeth (revised by Alice Mackrell). *History of 20th Century Fashion.* Hollywood, Calif.: Costume & Fashion Press, 2001.

MacKenzie, Mairi. *... Isms: Understanding Fashion.* London: Herbert Press, 2009.

Marsh, Lisa. *The House of Klein.* Hoboken, N.J.: John Wiley & Sons, Inc., 2003.

WEB SITES

Calvin Klein, Inc.
http://www.ck.com

The Fashion Encyclopedia
http://www.fashionencyclopedia.com/Ki-Le/Klein-Calvin.html

New York (magazine)
http://nymag.com/fashion/fashionshows/designers/bios/calvinklein/

The New York Times: Times Topics on Calvin Klein
http://topics.nytimes.com/topics/reference/timestopics/people/k/calvin_klein/

Style.com
http://www.style.com/fashionshows/designerdirectory/CKLEIN/seasons/

Picture Credits

Index

About the Author

MATT W. CODY is a writer who has been active in publishing for more than seven years. He is the author of *Peter Stuyvesant,* part of Chelsea House's LEADERS OF THE COLONIAL ERA titles. As an editor, he has been part of a number of educational programs in the fields of music, social studies, and reading/language arts, including Macmillan/McGraw-Hill's acclaimed *Spotlight on Music* program. He lives in New York City.